ATTENTION DEFICIT/ HYPERACTIVITY DISORDER

A Practical Guide for Teachers

PAUL COOPER
AND KATHERINE IDEUS

David Fulton Publishers

London

David Fulton Publishers Ltd
Ormond House, 26–27 Boswell Street, London WC1N 3JD

First published in Great Britain by
David Fulton Publishers 1996
Reprinted 1996 and 1997

Note: The right of the authors to be identified as the authors of their work has been asserted by them in accordance with the Copyright, Designs and Patents Act 1988.

Copyright © Paul Cooper and Katherine Ideus

British Library Cataloguing in Publication Data

A catalogue record for this book is available from the British Library

ISBN 1-85346-431-7

Typeset by Textype Typesetters, Cambridge
Printed in Great Britain by Bell & Bain Ltd

Contents

Dedication

To good teachers everywhere, especially:
Bill, Kathy, Fred and Monica.
Without whom this book would not have happened.

Preface: how to use this book

We have written this book with three main aims in mind:

- to provide basic information about the phenomenon that is Attention Deficit/Hyperactivity Disorder (AD/HD)
- to place AD/HD in the UK context
- to introduce teachers in the UK to the kinds of knowledge and understanding we believe to be most useful in dealing with AD/HD in schools

We have tried to do this in a style that is neither overly academic and theoretical, nor condescending. We have tried to communicate our understandings of AD/HD in a way that emphasises our compassion for the children who experience this disorder and our awareness of the intrinsic fascination that this subject presents to the interested observer. Clearly, we would like you to read this book and enjoy it. We would also like you to read this book and use it.

The chapters are each written in ways that attempt to answer the kinds of questions that teachers tend to raise about AD/HD. Each chapter is also followed by a summary of main points and a set of questions. We believe that this format will be useful to readers in that it will help them to develop knowledge of AD/HD whilst stimulating a critical response. We would also like this book to be used for school-based In Service Education for Teachers (INSET).

Unfortunately, as we write, the pool of resources to support teachers' continuing professional development in the UK is dwindling. This is particularly unfortunate at a time when there is a widespread concern at the increase in psycho-social disorders (such as rising crime rates among young people and declining standards of mental health) in our society that have a direct impact on the quality of the lives of children and teachers in classrooms. We regret this deeply. As educationists, (and as people having a parental interest in the UK state education system) we care about the quality of teaching and learning in schools.

We suggest that there are two main ways of using this book. (i) read it; use it; enjoy it and
(ii) adapt it for your own within school INSET, for example: organise a staff meeting around each chapter or part of a chapter, in which you discuss the questions we ask plus your own. A useful format for these meetings might be:

- 15 minute introduction in which a member of staff summarises main points of the chapter
- 20 minute discussion in small groups (of 4 or 5), which cover reactions to what has been read
- 15+ minute plenary in which all groups report back the key issues raised in their discussions

(iii) Decide what you and your school are going to do about AD/HD and other emotional and behavioural difficulties in your school in terms of (i) individual teacher response and (ii) whole school policy.

We thank you for looking at this book. We thank you for reading this book. But we really thank you for *using* this book.

Paul Cooper and Katherine Ideus
Cambridge University.
February, 1996

Introduction

Attention Deficit/Hyperactivity Disorder (AD/HD) is a complex and controversial subject. Unfortunately, to date, some of the popular debate about it has generated far more heat than light. This book attempts to offer a dispassionate account of the subject that will be of interest and value to teachers and parents who may be faced with a child having this condition.

Emotional and Behavioural Difficulties (EBD) and AD/HD

Since the early 1980s 'Emotional and Behavioural Difficulties' (EBD) has been a preferred term used by special educational professionals in the UK. EBD is an umbrella term used to describe children who display patterns of behaviour and/or emotional expression that have negative effects on (1) their own learning, and/or (2) the learning environment for other children. It is often stated (e.g. by Department for Education, circulars on 'Children with Problems', 1994) that the term EBD is most appropriately applied to problems that are seen as particularly 'serious' by teachers and/or parents. These problems are more serious than routine classroom misbehaviour, or normal emotional responses to temporarily stressful situations (e.g. anxiety at the prospect of public examinations), but not as serious as problems caused by psychiatric disturbance. The experience of most workers in the field is that in practical terms such distinctions are sometimes difficult to make. For example, what presents as routine classroom misbehaviour in one setting may escalate into something far more serious in another setting. The nature of the school environment and the quality of teachers' and other adults' understanding of EBDs and their remedies can sometimes make the difference between a child being considered 'manageable' and 'unmanageable'. This point might go some of the way to explaining occasionally puzzling variations in the numbers of exclusions reported by schools with similar pupil intakes.

Theorists and practitioners in the field often find it useful to distinguish between two broad categories of EBD: those which manifest themselves through *externalisation* and those which manifest themselves through *internalisation*. Externalised EBDs will often take the form of aggressive or 'acting out' behaviours, these may include physical and verbal aggression toward others, bullying, delinquency, apparent hyperactivity and other actively anti-social acts. Internalised EBDs more often take on the appearance of withdrawn behaviour, an unwillingness to communicate, a tendency to avoid social interaction and to be uncommunicative, anxiety and/or timidity: that is, asocial rather than anti-social behaviour.

The causes of EBD are many and varied. Broadly speaking they can be divided into two main categories: causes that are *within child* and causes that are *outside the child*. Generally speaking it is the causes that are outside the child that receive greatest attention. There are two good reasons for this.

1 Behavioural rather than Emotional Difficulties tend to be the most disruptive and distracting to teachers in schools, particularly those which involve oppositional and/or aggressive behaviour. These are the kinds of acts that disturb, threaten or frighten others and that might be roughly

equated with the kind of acts that committed in other settings might be deemed 'illegal'. By and large these acts (i.e. aggressive, anti-social, oppositional behaviour) are often seen as maladaptive behaviours (in the school setting) that have been learned, in the home, peer group or neighbourhood setting.

2 If maladaptive behaviours are learned then they can be unlearned, or rather, replaced by new learned behaviours. Successful schools and effective teachers are particularly good at influencing the behaviour of their pupils in positive ways.

The importance of *environment* in creating and alleviating behavioural problems should not be underestimated. It is nearly always of significant importance. However, it would be wrong to suggest that environment is the whole answer. Sometimes a child's behavioural problems are actually a symptom of another problem. For example, the child who is acting out in school may be reacting to a problem that is occurring elsewhere, such as in the family situation: a child who poses particular difficulties to specific teachers may be doing so as some kind of reaction to one of the adults in his or her home life. In this case the problem may be less usefully seen as behavioural, and more usefully seen as cognitive or emotional. In order to help a child in these circumstances a supportive and positive environment is necessary, but so too is cognitive training and/or counselling, with the aim of helping the child to develop new and more functional ways of thinking about how he or she behaves and/or coped with difficult feelings.

It is also important to recognise that that not all EBDs are *behavioural*. The child who is nearly always unhappy or apparently unfeeling, unusually withdrawn and unduly quiet, although not disruptive to the school process, may be expressing symptoms of the same kinds of emotional difficulties that cause some children to be oppositional and disruptive. Sometimes children with these kinds of problems are no trouble at all in the classroom, partly because they are rarely there (as in the case of school phobics), and because when they are there, they are utterly unobtrusive. If such a child is failing to make educational progress as a result of these difficulties then he or she has an educational difficulty of equal magnitude to the acting out child.

When it comes to *within child* factors, these can take the form of deep-seated emotional and psychological problems that have their origins in early childhood experiences, such as some forms of physical and emotional deprivation, neglect or abuse. Other traumatic events, such as bereavement, family break up or discord can also create patterns of thinking, feeling and behaving that make it very difficult for the child to adjust to circumstances that other children adapt to easily. Another form of within child factor is that which is related to the child's *biological make up*.

There are many biological factors that can influence our emotional and behavioural reactions. Most of us are familiar with the ways in which our moods can be influenced by normal and natural variations in the chemical activity of our bodies, such as those that occur as a result of changes in hormone or blood-sugar levels. Some of these effects can be simulated through the use of certain chemicals, such as alcohol, caffeine, nicotine, or medication of some kind. Certain forms of clinical depression are associated with biochemical activities in the brain. Similarly, particular patterns of brain activity have been associated with certain forms of social, emotional and behavioural problems. One of the most obvious of these is *autism*. Others include *Asperger's syndrome* and *Tourette's syndrome*. People suffering from these conditions often have marked difficulty in relating to other people in ways that are generally regarded as socially acceptable, and they can sometimes behave in ways that most people find alarming or socially disruptive. These conditions are increasingly seen as having a genetic basis, though some of the neurological conditions that are associated with their symptomology can be produced as a result of injuries to the brain.

One such condition is *Attention Deficit/Hyperactivity Disorder*. It is important to address this issue in a publication such as this because of the increasing belief, among a growing body parents and professionals, that a far larger number of people are affected by this condition than has been previously thought.

The rest of this book will be devoted to an exploration of some of the key aspects of AD/HD, with a view to helping teachers understand and cope with the condition more effectively in the classroom. It will become clear, as the book unfolds, that there are many dimensions to AD/HD. The book will provide an account of current theory about the nature of AD/HD. In keeping with the clinical and research literature, it will be argued that children with AD/HD differ from the majority of children within the same developmental stage in their abilities to (1) control their impulses; (2) focus their attention; and, in some cases (3) control their motor activity.

There are a number of important things to bear in mind about within child factors:

- **Biology can and does account for some genuine and important differences between people**

It is a truism to suggest that all people are unique. We vary in many ways from one another in terms of our physical and temperamental make up, tendencies and needs. For example biological differences do make some things easier or more difficult for some of us than others. The constructed world we live in is built around certain beliefs about the way that most people are. For example, if one is of a certain height one may find travelling on public transport uncomfortable, possibly because one is too short to reach the hanging straps, or too tall to stand up straight in a tube train. Among the basic ideas underpinning this book is the idea that certain mental tendencies are differentially distributed among the population, rather like height. It will be suggested that the child who suffers from AD/HD has a lesser capacity for sustaining attention and controlling certain impulses than most people of the same developmental level. This capacity is believed to have a biological basis. Because schools and many other aspects of our world are designed to cater specifically for the majority of people whose attention and impulse control capacities fall within a range that is greater than that of the child with AD/HD, this child experiences difficulties in coping with situations that most people deal with very effectively.

● Biology is not destiny

Although, theoretically, we can think of individuals' capacities to control their impulses, sustain attention and regulate motor activity as being differentially distributed, rather like height, we must be very careful with this analogy. Unlike height we do not have precise and universal means of measuring an individual's level of impulse control. Furthermore, we do not have a precise means for identifying the *extent* to which an individual's capacities in these areas are rooted in his or her biology or are the result of other factors (for example environmental influences).

In addition to this, human beings are often very successful in developing strategies to help them overcome biological difficulties. For example, people with hearing impairment may learn to lip read and use sign language; visually impaired people will sometimes employ touch and hearing to access information that fully sighted people process visually. More prosaically, people sometimes employ cosmetic strategies (e.g. clothing; make-up) to disguise biological 'facts' about their age, weight or height. Furthermore, as a society, we impose laws and other forms of control and support to protect individuals from being socially disadvantaged as a result of biological differences (e.g. legislation on race and sex discrimination, and special educational needs).

This means that just because someone has a difficulty, like AD/HD, it does not infer that they are doomed to failure or that we should have low expectations of their performance. Information about a difficulty should be seen as an aid to enabling the individual to succeed; not as an excuse for failure or neglect. To put this more strongly: once we have an understanding of the nature of a condition such as AD/HD we have a responsibility to act on this knowledge to facilitate *positive* outcomes.

● Biological and other individual differences often highlight problems that affect everyone

Problems like AD/HD or sensory impairment affect some people severely, some people moderately, and some people mildly. The significance of this point is that many of the interventions that are appropriate in meeting the needs of children with AD/HD benefit virtually all children. An example of this is the way in which children with AD/HD appear to benefit from having regular activity breaks. One study found that when hyperactive children were given regular activity breaks, between cognitive tasks lasting for about 45 minutes, their own task behaviour and concentration increased considerably and they displayed virtually no hyperactive behaviours during tasks. Clearly, all children in our schools would and do benefit when care is taken over the ways in which time is allocated. Research studies of schools in the western world over the last 30 years have repeatedly pointed to the relationship between the ways schools are organised and pupil disaffection and disruption. Where teachers and schools consider all their pupils' needs for a variety of engaging and stimulating experience, as well their needs for structure, security and individual expression there seem to be much lower levels of disharmony and disruption, as well as improved learning outcomes.

This is not to say that the needs of a child who is severely affected with

AD/HD will always be met in exactly the same way as for all other children. As this book will show, there are sometimes special measures that need to be taken to meet the individual needs of the child with AD/HD, that relate to the specific nature of the condition. What is being said here is that AD/HD can make a child hypersensitive to conditions that other children may be able to tolerate to different degrees. When efforts are made to address the problems that MOST disturb children with AD/HD, the learning environment for ALL children is enhanced because most of the measures involved focus on minimising factors that impede learning, and maximising those that make learning accessible.

AD/HD and Medicine

AD/HD is a medical diagnosis, and as such can only be made by a physician. It should also be stressed, however, that effective assessment and treatment of the condition always involves teachers and parents centrally. The stimulant medication methylphenidate (brand name: 'Ritalin') is often prescribed by doctors for this condition. The function of medication is to help the child to concentrate and, therefore, take advantage of learning opportunities in school. If a child's performance is in any way impaired by the medication, then it is likely that the dosage is inappropriate and should be reviewed by the doctor.

The child with AD/HD

The fact that AD/HD is a medical diagnosis can be problematic for the schoolteacher. Clearly, for the doctor a child's medical condition is the primary concern. The patient in the hospital ward, although believing him- or herself to be a complex and fascinating human being, may actually be thought of by the doctor (and referred to) as 'the 'irritable bowel syndrome in cubicle three'. This is not necessarily a criticism of the medical profession. The medical practitioner's interest in, and responsibility towards, the patient is primarily medical.

In the school setting, however, there is no such thing as 'the AD/HD child' or 'the ADD child'. There are only children *with* AD/HD. This is an important point to make at the outset because it is easy to use labels like AD/HD in ways that are not educationally useful. If we are to help children with AD/HD to benefit from schooling we must remember that they are first and foremost children, and our responsibility to them is to create the best circumstances for their educational development. The fact that they have possible AD/HD is only of interest to us in so far as it helps us to help them to be successful in school. We should avoid using AD/HD as an *excuse* for failure or underperformance. When AD/HD is used as an excuse it can be disabling, because it may be taken to indicate a hopeless situation. It is preferable to see AD/HD as a positive reason, or justification for a modification or intervention that is *enabling*. Thus, as a rule AD/HD should be used not as a *reason for not* doing something, but as a *reason for doing* something positive.

Some problems with medical diagnoses and educational problems

In preceding sections we described the way in which we believe AD/HD should be seen as a subcategory of the all-embracing term 'Emotional and

Behavioural Difficulties'. Unfortunately, this is not the way in which the condition is sometimes portrayed. There has been a tendency among some writers and practitioners to treat the two terms as oppositional. There are three possible reasons for this:

(1) Until relatively recently, the AD/HD diagnosis was not widely known among educational professionals in the UK.

(2) Historically the EBD category developed partly as a result of the ways in which ideas about learning difficulties have changed over the years. Important developments in the 1950s, 1960s and 1970s gave educational psychologists and teachers increasing importance in determining the educational provision for children who in the early years of state education were defined in medical terms as 'handicapped' or 'educationally subnormal'. It was (in our view) rightly argued that these medicalised labels defined individuals in terms of their deficits, rather than their positive potential. The whole thrust of educational psychology throughout this past 40 years has been to shift the emphasis from deficit to *needs*. The law now supports the simple but powerful view that we should not use a child's physical, behavioural or cognitive disabilities as excuses for excluding him or her from entitlement to the state-funded education enjoyed by the majority, but rather, these 'disabilities' should be seen as 'difficulties' in accessing state education that it is the responsibility of government and LEA's to overcome. The emphasis, therefore, has shifted from the individual child's difficulties to the systems that are set up to educate all children. The argument now goes something like: as educators, we don't need to know what is 'wrong' with the child, we simply need to know what we can do to help the child to learn, and, if possible, do so in a mainstream school. This is why the emphasis of special needs education is now on 'learning difficulties' *per se*, as opposed to different categories of disability or handicap.

(3) Provision for children with Special Educational Needs (SEN) as well as the availability of knowledge and expertise among teachers working with children with SEN have been affected by the abandonment of the medical model. The welcome tendency towards inclusive education has led to a decrease in the availability of off-site specialist facilities for children with SEN, and an emphasis on the training of Special Educational Needs Co-ordinators in schools as generalists in SEN, rather than specialists in any particular area.

These developments, whilst having many positive effects, have also had some less welcome consequences. The move away from individualised explanations of EBD has led to an overwhelming emphasis on environmental explanations. The first resort of UK professionals confronted with a child who exhibits emotional and/or behavioural problems is to seek an explanation which locates the cause of the problem in the child's family or school environment. If parents or teachers offer 'within child' explanations, they are likely, in some cases, to be dismissed as seeking to avoid taking responsibility for the situation. Whilst it is clearly often the case that EBD is exacerbated or even sometimes created by adverse environmental circumstances (in the home, school or wider community) the case of AD/HD shows us that sometimes there are within child problems which need to be addressed directly if changes in the environment are to have any appreciable effect.

For these reasons it has been difficult for some UK professionals to accept the AD/HD diagnosis. Our view is, however, that these difficulties are essentially cultural. That is to say, there are certain ways of thinking about things, such as emotional and/or behavioural problems, which differ from one setting to another. These differences lead to problems of communication when people from one setting try to speak to people from another. AD/HD cuts across many cultural boundaries. In particular it cuts across disciplinary boundaries, between teachers and medical professionals, and national boundaries: originating in the USA, and being presented to a UK audience. In the case of AD/HD these misunderstandings tend to revolve around issues of the extent to which behavioural problems may or may not relate to within child factors. The underlying argument of this book is that we need to look beyond surface, cultural differences. We hope to show that when we do this we find that AD/HD is a very useful concept to the teacher in that it helps him or her to provide more effective educational opportunities to certain children. We suggest that one important message to be taken from the case of AD/HD is that the kinds of problems that AD/HD presents are not simply a product of biology, but are the result of a complex interaction between the child's biology and his or her experience of the environment. This means that the child with AD/HD will often need interventions that address his or her biological differences as well as interventions that involve the provision of certain experiences and environmental conditions. AD/HD is not an imported fad. AD/HD is a useful tool, knowledge of which, when added to the UK teacher's existing armoury of strategies for dealing with EBD, will help teachers to become yet more effective in helping children to learn.

This book

The rest of this book is concerned with what teachers need to know and do about Attention Deficit/Hyperactivity Disorder (AD/HD). The book is divided into six chapters, each of which deals with questions that we have been asked by teachers about this condition during the course of the many training sessions we have conducted on this topic over the past two years. The six areas dealt with are:

- the nature of AD/HD
- the assessment of AD/HD
- approaching AD/HD from the teacher perspective
- interventions that teachers can use to help children with AD/HD
- the role of medication in the treatment of AD/HD
- special issues and concerns relating to AD/HD

At the end of the book is an appendix section, which includes:

- a glossary of terms relating to AD/HD
- a further reading section
- a list of relevant addresses and resources

This is one of the first books written specifically for teachers in the UK. It is, therefore, presented as an introductory text. The book is based upon extensive research in the literature as well as experience with, and research among, parents, professionals and children. We know how busy teachers are, however, and for that reason we have attempted to present the information in this book in as succinct and accessible a form as we can*.

We hope you find this book interesting, informative and useful. We hope that it will stimulate discussion and reflection on practice, as well as further reading and research. More than anything, we hope that this book will make at least a small contribution to improving the educational experience of vulnerable children, both with and without AD/HD.

---

* In the interests of accessibility, brevity and readability we have kept references to other publications out of the text as far as possible. We have cited key sources in the 'Further Reading' section. Readers who wish to explore this fascinating topic further may wish to read our earlier publication which deals with AD/HD in greater depth. This is: Paul Cooper and Katherine Ideus (editors): *Attention Deficit/Hyperactivity Disorder: Educational, Medical and Cultural Issues*, East Sutton: Association of Workers for Children with Emotional and Behavioural Difficulties Copies can be purchased from Allan Rimmer (Administrative Officer), Charlton Court, East Sutton, Nr. Maidstone, Kent.

CHAPTER 1

What is AD/HD and where does it come from?

What is AD/HD?

Attention Deficit/Hyperactivity Disorder (AD/HD) is a medical diagnosis that is applied to children and adults who are experiencing significant behavioural and cognitive difficulties in important aspects of their lives (e.g. in their familial and personal relationships; at school or work). These difficulties can be attributed to problems of impulse control, hyperactivity and inattention. A type of Attention Deficit Disorder without hyperactivity has also been identified. It is believed that these problems are caused primarily by dysfunctions in the frontal lobes of the brain that are most likely genetically transmitted.

The AD/HD diagnosis was devised by the American Psychiatric Association (APA). It should be noted that there is a similar diagnosis, devised by the World Health Organisation (WHO), that is already well established in Europe. The WHO diagnosis is referred to as Hyperkinetic Disorder. The major difference between the WHO diagnosis and the APA diagnosis is that the WHO condition focuses entirely on extreme levels of hyperactivity as the main presenting problem, and, unlike the APA version, does not have a non-hyperactive subtype. There are also particular differences in the ways in which the two sets of diagnostic criteria: (1) were derived, (2) the degree to which the diagnosis is dependent on the exhibition of symptoms across a range of circumstances, and (3) the specificity of symptom descriptions to particular circumstances. For these reasons hyperkinetic syndrome is best seen as a subset of the broader AD/HD diagnosis.

What AD/HD looks like in the classroom

Children with AD/HD are often of average to high ability, but disturb their parents and teachers because their classroom achievement is erratic, and often below their apparent level of ability.

The child with AD/HD will often be a source of exasperation to the teacher. The child may show, on some occasions high levels of performance, a ready wit and an imagination of a high order. The problem is that the child's performance is erratic. In one manifestation of the disorder he or she may often appear disengaged, be easily distracted and unmotivated. The child may often appear to be lazy. In another major manifestation, the child will appear to be wasting obvious ability in favour of being oppositional and disruptive: often out of his or her seat; bothering classmates; often off task.

Children with AD/HD will tend to fall into one of three subtypes: (1) AD/HD, predominantly inattentive type: those who are mainly distracted and inattentive, (2) AD/HD, predominantly hyperactive-impulsive type, and (3) AD/HD, combined type: those who combine hyperactivity with inattention and distractibility. These children are frustrating to teach because of their unpredictability, their failure to conform to expectations and their tendency to 'not learn from their mistakes'. These are the children who often hear the following complaints and questions from their teachers and parents:

'If I've told you once, I've told you a thousand times: DON'T DO THAT! Why can't you learn to do as you are told - like most other people?'
'Why do you always have to be the one to get it wrong?'
'Why is it that you are always one of the ones who doesn't hand in their homework?'

To make matters worse, the child's often honest answer to these questions is remarkably consistent: 'I don't know'. The problem is, that as the child gets older and moves into the secondary phase, the years of exasperation and blame can also lead to disaffection. So that the child with AD/HD, if not handled appropriately, may not only continue to have difficulties in concentration and impulse control that are basically biological in nature, he or she may also develop an antipathy to school and a lack of motivation to even try to overcome his or her difficulties.

The details of the diagnosis, as applied to schoolchildren, are that individual difficulties in the school environment and/or in the family setting are associated with various combinations of some of the following characteristics.

Inattention

- Children with AD/HD differ from their peers in the degree to which they appear to be able to sustain attention in tasks and play activities.
- They appear to be more easily distracted from tasks and play activities than their peers.
- They will also display extreme difficulties in starting and finishing schoolwork and other activities.
- They show a greater tendency than their peers to be inattentive and appear to ignore or find it impossible to follow instructions.
- They may also appear to be unusually disorganised and forgetful for their age.

Hyperactivity

- Their hyperactivity will manifest itself in unusually high levels of fidgetting, and unauthorised movement in the classroom situation or other situations where it is deemed inappropriate to roam freely.
- They will also show a greater tendency than their peers to want to run around and be 'on the go'.
- They are often noisy and over talkative, when compared with their peers.

Impulsivity

- Their impulsivity manifests itself in an over tendency to interrupt others, to butt into conversations, to have difficulty in waiting for their turn to participate in games or answer questions in class.

The onset of the disorder is signalled by the presence of some of these symptoms before the age of 7 years (APA, 1994; WHO, 1990. See the resource section at end of this book for copies of the formal diagnostic criteria.)

It should be stressed that these symptoms are present to a degree that they interfere significantly with the individual's functioning, often to the extent of leading to failure in school or in professional, personal and social life.

The mainly hyperactive subtype

Where hyperactivity is present, the child is likely to show marked antisocial tendencies, to be actively rejected by peers and runs a high risk of suspension from school or referral to special educational needs provision.

The mainly inattentive subtype

Where hyperactivity is not present, the child's behaviour is likely to be more marked by a tendency to daydream and appear sluggish. Such children are also more likely to internalise problems. They tend to be neglected rather than rejected by peers, and are likely to display learning difficulties.

What the child with AD/HD looks like in the classroom

The classroom behaviour of children with AD/HD is often marked by some or all of the following:

- Being out of seat too frequently
- Deviating from what the rest of the class is supposed to be doing
- Not following teacher's instructions or orders
- Talking out of turn or calling out
- Being aggressive toward classmates
- Having a short attention span and being distractible
- Bothering classmates by talking to them or intruding on their work efforts
- Being oblivious and daydreaming
- Losing and forgetting equipment
- Handing in homework late or not at all
- Handing in incomplete or sloppy work (Based on J. Taylor, 1994)

What it feels like to have AD/HD

It is often the case that children with AD/HD experience the world as a hostile place. In early infancy children with AD/HD are often fractious. For no apparent reason they may cry to an extreme degree and have difficulty sleeping. In some cases they appear to find physical contact distressing to the extent that they resist parents' attempts to cuddle them, or show strong aversions to certain fabrics, tastes or textures. They may also be hypersensitive to other sensory stimuli, and react with discomfort to levels of sound and light that others find tolerable. Sometimes children with

AD/HD appear to show little understanding of or empathy for the feelings of others. This can manifest itself in cruelty to peers or pets. Such cruelty is often committed, however, without malice so that the child fails to understand the reason why he or she is punished, or other children are rejecting following their act of cruelty.

As children get older we tend to have increasingly high expectations of them. For example, we expect to be able to give them increasingly complex instructions and for them to carry them out. A problem that children with AD/HD often experience is the failure to be able to grasp and recall even relatively short sequences of instructions, such as:

'When the bell goes, go to your form room, pick up your homework diary and take it to your head of year. Your head of year will be in his or her classroom.'

Children with AD/HD often have difficulty with auditory processing, that is, they may have perfectly good hearing and hear the instruction, but they are impaired in their ability to extract understanding from the sounds they hear. They also tend to be forgetful and easily distracted.

For these reasons the experience of AD/HD has sometimes been likened to being in a fog. The child is aware that there are things going on around him or her but those things often remain indistinct and only half recognised. Another useful analogy is that having AD/HD is rather like being a radio receiver that is badly tuned in, so that rather than receiving one signal or station clearly, several signals are being picked up simultaneously, with the result that the information being received is jumbled and difficult to make sense of. The way this is experienced in the classroom can be illustrated by the following sequence.

What the child with AD/HD looks like in the classroom

1. One minute the child with AD/HD is listening to the teacher's instructions;
2. the child becomes distracted by an event that most other people are able to ignore (e.g. another child drops a book);
3. if the child is also hyperactive, he or she may be tapping and fidgeting.
4. The teacher finishes his or her instructions,
5. and the child with AD/HD is again distracted by the movement of the rest of the class, most of whom are complying with the teacher's instructions.
6. The child with AD/HD, however, because he or she has only received a part of the instructions is now bewildered and uncertain about what he or she should be doing.
7. The child cannot do the task and may well be punished as a result.

What it feels like to have AD/HD

Bewilderment, uncertainty, repeated rebukes for laziness and the stigma of failure often have a demoralising affect on the child. The problem is the child with AD/HD is often punished, blamed or otherwise negated for behaviour over which they have little control. They are constantly told off for behaviour that they cannot help. This can often lead to low self-esteem, conduct problems and a lack of motivation, which will go on to exacerbate their existing problems. In short, if mishandled the child with AD/HD may well become the lazy, unmotivated child that he or she has been unjustly labelled as. They are often children who have tried their best, failed, and then been blamed for not trying.

Primary and Secondary effects of AD/HD

The symptoms of AD/HD are problems that many children and adults (if not all) have from time to time. The child with AD/HD, however, stands out from the rest of the class because he or she presents many of these problems to a far greater extent than the rest of the class. In fact, for children with AD/HD these problems are so chronic and persistent that they interfere with their daily lives, and, often, the lives of those around them to a severe extent.

These are children who stand out from the others because of their persistence in failing to conform. Their AD/HD may manifest itself in their repeated failure to follow instructions with which other children readily comply. Such as the child who persistently fails to produce homework always with the same excuse: 'I forgot to do it'. Another example might be the child who can be relied upon to turn any group work task into a verbal or physical punch up. This is the child who, when you anounce he or she is to join blue group for the role play exercise, inspires a loud cheer from pink, green, black and grey groups, and despairing groans from the members of blue group. This is the child who 'always spoils everything', in situations where most children learn to cooperate. The child with AD/HD might also, however, be the child who never gets noticed: the child whose name you can never quite recall; the child who is always in a dream.

These children may be a source of frustration and anxiety to their peers, their parents and their teachers. As a result they may be rejected or ignored by their peers, and, in some cases, by their parents and teachers (or schools). Whatever the outcome, however, children with these problems place enormous strain on the people with whom they live and interact. They are difficult to parent, difficult to teach and difficult to be friends with. This in turn can have a secondary effect on the child with AD/HD, who may get to feel unwanted, uncared for and generally misunderstood. So often, because their problems are considered to be deficiencies in effort and motivation, the constant failures associated with them depress pupils' self- esteem and make them prone to even further failure. Leaving the child 'depressed, discouraged and disheartened' (Taylor, 1994).

There are, therefore, *primary* effects of AD/HD, that affect the indiviual's social and cognitive functioning in the classroom, as well as interfering with the activities of others. There are also *secondary* effects of AD/HD that derive largely from the ways in which people around the AD/HD sufferer treat him or her. Because people with AD/HD are often misunderstood, and believed to be deliberately uncooperative, rude or oppositional, they tend to be rejected in one way or another by those around them. This in turn may lead to emotional problems, in the form of low self-esteem and withdrawn behaviour. It may also lead to conduct disorder, as a result of resentment on the part of the child who is constantly being blamed and punished for behaviour over which he or she has little or no control.

Socialised EBD or AD/HD?

As we stated in the introduction to this book, AD/HD should properly be seen, in the UK context, as a subcategory of the Special Education

5

umberella term of 'Emotional and Behavioural Difficulties' (EBD). An important point to note is that there are many surface similarities between AD/HD and what we might refer to as socialised Emotional and Behavioural Difficulties. By socialised EBD we mean those EBDs that are the result of some trauma in the child's life, such as family dischord or break-up, poor parenting, social deprivation, abuse and bereavement.

The key point of the AD/HD diagnosis is that it should only be applied when the symptoms present themselves both in school, in the home and when they have serious consequences for the quality of life of the child and/or the other people involved. After all, everyone displays some AD/HD characteristics some of the time, but it is only very few people for whom these characteristics are harmful to their everyday functioning, to the extent that they create serious long-term difficulties in relationships with others and in carrying out domestic and work or school-related tasks.

Particular characteristics of the AD/HD diagnosis that distinguish it from socialised EBD are:

- AD/HD is considered to be a *lifelong* condition carried, in some form, into adulthood by, it its estimated between 30 and 70 per cent of people diagnosed in childhood
- AD/HD is believed to have a *biological basis*, in that it is probably caused to a significant degree by dysfunctions of the neurotransmitters in the frontal lobes of the brain
- AD/HD focuses entirely on behaviour
- An important part of the treatment for AD/HD is often stimulant and other forms of *medication*

Important commonalities between AD/HD and socialised EBD are as follows.

- Children with AD/HD or socialised EBD experience difficulty in doing things that other children do relatively easily, especially conforming to the kinds of behavioural expectations that are common in schools. Their behaviour is rooted in circumstances beyond their immediate control.
- Because children with AD/HD or socialised EBD experience social and educational failure they have low self esteem. Therefore, they often do not believe that they are capable of meeting the challenges that schools face them with and become trapped in a repeating cycle of failure.
- There are skills associated with good behaviour, just as there are skills associated with school subjects. Pupils with AD/HD or socialised EBD need to be taught what good behaviour is and how to do it.

Pseudo-AD/HD

There are circumstances in which socialised EBD may look just like AD/HD. For example, a child may show symptoms of impulsivity, inattentiveness and/or hyperactivity in ways that appear to conform to the description of the condition as supplied in the diagnostic criteria. However, this is only AD/HD if the symptoms can be shown to have:

(1) lasted for at least 6 months

(2) been expressed at a high level of intensity, that

(3) is clearly having a severely adverse effect on the child's social and cognitive functioning in the family and at school, and

(4) have been in evidence since before the age of 7 years.

If the symptoms do not conform with any one of these conditions then the the problem is unlikely to be the neurologically based problem that is AD/HD. This is more likely to be *pseudo-AD/HD* (Hallowell and Ratey, 1995) which is better understood as *socialised EBD*.

It is important to make this distinction because the two different conditions often have different implications for action. Pseudo-AD/HD is likely to be a response to a specific, non-constitutional condition. For example, a child may be inattentive, impulsive and/or hyperactive in response to a family problem, such as bereavement, or because of changes in family circumstances (divorce; problems with step-parents or siblings). There may be deep-seated psychological problems that relate to experiences of neglect or abuse. A child may experience depression and anxiety that are related to any number of personal and situational changes that occur in the course of everyday life. Similarly, a child may exhibit some of these behaviours as a way of acting out feelings of frustration and anxiety in the face of what are perceived by him or her to be hostile influences in the school, home or peer group situation.

Some of these problems are clearly more deep seated and long term than others. They are all serious problems that require intervention of some sort. Often, however, the interventions required involve dealing with the cause of the problem. Where a child is psychologically upset, it is often appropriate to offer counselling in an attempt to help the child come to terms with difficult emotions. Similarly, by creating a more supportive and caring environment a child's esteem problems may be addressed more effectively. Behavioural therapy is also a useful way of helping children to learn appropriate ways of behaving and of expressing themslves.

The symptoms of AD/HD may be *exacerbated* by the kinds of stressors noted above, therefore, some of these approaches can help the child with AD/HD. However, they are seldom sufficient on their own. The child with AD/HD is not likely to conform readily to the behavioural expectations that are appropriate for most children without very specific account being taken of the special nature of the condition. For example, whilst it is important to deal with the secondary effects of AD/HD on a child's self-esteem, by helping him or her to focus cognitively on his or her positive achievements rather than failures, it is unlikely that such an approach alone will help the child to behave differently. The child with AD/HD who displays hyperactivity as a primary symptom is not hyperactive out of choice, or because of a particular set of perceptions that he or she holds about the classroom situation. The hyperactivity is the result of a neurological impairment that makes the control of motor activity constitutionally difficult for the child. Classroom interventions alone, such as behavioural therapy or counselling, will not be effective in changing hyperactive behaviour that is so caused. Effective interventions for AD/HD seek less to change behaviour than to *manage* it, for example, by minimising extraneous stimulation, or creating opportunities for hyperactivity to be expressed in ways that do not interfere with the classroom situation (such as frequent activity breaks). Similarly, children who are constitutionally inattentive, are also likely to be forgetful and not as receptive as most to 'talking therapies', simply because of the difficulties they have with discriminating, attending to and retaining auditory stimuli. This is not say that some forms of talking therapy might not work provided they are supported by accommodations, such as training in mnemonic strategies to assist with recall.

Importance of rigorous and effective assessment procedures

AD/HD is a very specific problem, requiring very specific responses so it is vitally important that the diagnosis is based on a thorough and detailed assessment process. A detailed account of what this process looks like is given in Chapter 2. Stated briefly, this process depends on gathering data from a wide range of sources about the child's functioning in different circumstances. Such assessment cannot be carried out over the space of a short visit to a single clinician. Effective assessment always requires the involvement of a multidisciplinary team which includes the parents, the child, a medical doctor, a psychologist, a social worker and teachers. Only with the involvement of all of these perspectives will it be possible to rule out all the other possible causes of the child's symptoms and so leave the clinician with AD/HD as the only explanation for the problems.

Overlaps between AD/HD and other emotional/behavioural and learning problems

Research from the USA shows that children with AD/HD also tend to have other emotional and behavioural difficulties that are not in themselves necessarily related directly to AD/HD, but may interact with the AD/HD to intensify learning and adjustment problems. Studies indicate the overlap between AD/HD and the following problems:

- 60 per cent of children with AD/HD display oppositional and defiant behaviour (e.g. often losing temper, arguing with adults, refusing to comply, deliberately annoying others) to a degree that is severely disruptive;
- 45 per cent of children with AD/HD display conduct disorder (chronic aggression towards others, destructive behaviour, deceitfulness or theft, serious and chronic rule breaking) to a severe degree;
- 25 per cent of children with AD/HD display antisocial or delinquent (i.e. criminal) behaviour;
- 30 per cent of children with AD/HD display clinically defined anxiety disorders;
- 33 per cent of children with AD/HD experience major clinical depression;
- 50 per cent + children with AD/HD display emotional problems;
- 50 per cent + children with AD/HD show social skills problems.

In addition. children with AD/HD tend to exhibit the following learning problems:

- 90 per cent of children with AD/HD are underproductive in schoolwork;
- 90 per cent of children with AD/HD underachieve in school;

- 20 per cent of children with AD/HD have reading difficulties;
- 60 per cent of children with AD/HD have serious handwriting difficulties;
- 30 per cent of children with AD/HD drop out of school in the USA;
- 5 per cent of people with AD/HD complete a 4-year degree course in a college or university in the USA, compared with approximately 25 per cent of the general population.

As has been already suggested, some of the problems associated with AD/HD, such as poor motivation and low self esteem may be *secondary effects* of the condition, that is: problems that are the result of the ways in which the primary problems associated with the disorder (poor attention, impulsivity and hyperactivity) are inappropriately dealt with by parents and teachers.

Causes of AD/HD

At the present time AD/HD is believed to be caused primarily by neurological dysfunction. Current theory suggests that the characteristic problems of AD/HD (i.e. lack of implulse control, chronic inattentiveness and hyperactivity) have their roots in a disorder located in the frontal lobes of the brain. A major function of this part of the brain is to control our impulses and regulate the ways in which we direct our attention. Research studies have found particularly low levels of activity in the neurotransmitters in this part of the brain among AD/HD sufferers. It is for this reason that stimulant medication has proven to be very useful in the treatment of this condition, since the effects of such medication are to increase activity between neurotransmitters.

This explanation of the nature of AD/HD helps to underline the key point that the condition is not, primarily, a problem of 'motivation', as educators normally use this word (i.e. meaning 'consciously choosing to apply effort'). A good analogy here is cerebral palsy (CP). CP is a neurological condition that affects the individual's ability to control his or her muscle and limb movements. Children with CP are prone to involuntary movements of their limbs, in the same way that children with AD/HD are prone to involuntary shifts of their attention; involuntary expressions of their impulses, and involuntary motor activity.

It is important to note at this point, however, that the term 'motivation' is a complex one. Neuroscientists often use this word in a slightly different way to teachers. In this other usage the term is taken to mean an individual's internal drive toward a specific action. In this sense there is nothing necessarily voluntary about 'motivation'. In fact, a failure of motivation in these circumstances is often the result of a dysfunction in the drive system. This means that in the case of AD/HD, it is technically correct to say that the child is not 'motivated' to pay attention, because the neurological system that stimulates most individuals to direct and focus their attention is underfunctioning. This is an important point to make, because it may be the case that the different professionals involved may use this important word in different and even contradictory ways: the one using it to describe conscious, willful, deliberate behaviour, and the other to describe drive mechanisms that are outside conscious control.

The causes of this particular brain dysfunction in most cases appear to be *genetic*. Research studies have found that in approximately 70 per cent of cases the neurology is inherited. Between 20 and 30 per cent of cases are caused by one of the following environmental factors:

- **brain disease:** such as encephalitis
- **brain injury:** as a result of physical trauma to the head
- **toxin exposure:** as a result of alcohol or drug abuse; exposure to lead. This can happen at both pre- and post-natal stages.

Of course, because there is a powerful genetic component it is very likely that the child with AD/HD will reflect traits that are present in one or both parents. This may inevitably lead to the 'obvious' conclusion that the child's problems are the result of socialisation. Clearly, where the genetic component is present in both the child and an immediate parent there will be *both* a genetic *and* a socialised component. In these circumstances the child will not only have to be helped to overcome geneticially inherited difficulties, he or she will also have to be helped to learn new patterns of behaviour that may well conflict with those learned in the home situation. Having said this, it is important to realise that the genetic transmission of traits (such as hair and eye colour, height, and mannerisms) can often skip a generation or more, so that physical and behavioural resemblances can be greater between children and other relatives than between children and parents.

- **So You Think *You've* Got AD/HD: Incidence of the Condition**

If you have read up to this point in the book you should have a pretty good idea what AD/HD is and what it is not. You may even be thinking that you actually *have it*! And even if you don't, there are large numbers of your family and the children you teach who have it. At this point we should reassure you that you *probably* do *not* have it, and that the vast majority of the children you teach *probably* do not have it (unless you teach in a setting that caters specifically for children with AD/HD or Hyperkinetic Syndrome). Remember anyway that this book is *not* a diagnostic tool: it is merely a guide to help you learn more about this issue. Diagnosis should only be made by an informed physician, and only on the basis of rigorous multi-disciplinary assessment.

At the present time it is estimated that between 3 and 5 per cent of *all people* in the USA have AD/HD, whilst up to *7 per cent of children* in the USA have it. No comparable figures on AD/HD are available in the UK. Large-scale studies of children in the UK, however, indicate that 1 per cent of children experience *Hyperkinetic Syndrome*, which is a World Health Organisation diagnosis that has a more restricitive diagnostic criteria than AD/HD. Hyperkinetic Syndrome is, in effect, a subcategory of AD/HD, which is applied to children who exhibit extreme hyperactivity. On the basis of American research we can assume that at least 1 per cent of children in the UK suffer from ADD without hyperactivity. If we further consider the fact that the AD/HD diagnostic criteria is less restrictive than the WHO criteria, we would expect the incidence of AD/HD to be more than 2 per cent at the very minimum. We would further suggest that the incidence is *probably* higher than this: possibly 3 per cent or more, when we take into account the findings of USA studies. One of the reasons for this is the suggestion that ADD without hyperactivity (mainly inattentive type) is often underdiagnosed. This underdiagnosis is often attributed to the fact that although chronic inattentiveness can cause severe learning problems, it does not tend to lead to openly disruptive behaviour. The child whose main problem is a lack of attentiveness will, rather than disrupt lessons, fade away into the background and be ignored by both teachers and peers. It is the case that girls are more likely to be affected by ADD without hyperactivity than boys. This fact may go some of the way to explaining why four times as many boy as girls receive the AD/HD diagnosis in the USA. The likelihood is that many girls and some boys with the inattentive version of AD/HD go unnoticed, though they suffer severe, social, emotional and educational consequences of the disorder. The 3 per cent figure is, therefore, a cautious and probably conservative figure, on the basis of existing evidence.

This means that, on average, *at least one child is every class of 30 has AD/HD*. So although you probably do not have AD/HD you do probably know at least one student who does, and the likelihood is that you know many more. Although only a relatively small number of people have the condition themselves, they affect the lives of many others as a consequence of their difficulties. They also need the help and support of many people to make changes and achieve success,

Why the sudden AD/HD epidemic? A brief history of AD/HD

As a reader of this book in the 1990s you would be forgiven for thinking that AD/HD is a new phenomenon. It is not. There is in fact a 200-year history to the idea that certain behavioural difficulties may have their basis in physiological rather than social or moral origins. If we look at the present century we find that in 1902 a British medical doctor (Still) reported, in *The Lancet*, on a group of children whose behaviour was characterised by a tendency to be: 'passionate, deviant, spiteful and lacking inhibitory volition.' The important issue here is that there was no indication of parental or other environmental causation. Still hypothesised mild brain injury as the cause. A growing body of research supporting the biological basis for some behavioural problems was strengthened by observations of the effects of the world-wide epidemic of viral encephalitis (a disease affecting the brain) which occurred in 1917. It was found that the infection left some children impaired in the areas of attention, memory and impulse control. In 1926 a British physician, Head, presented the theory that specific brain damage was directly related to certain language disorders. In 1936 Werner, and later Blau, related behavioural disturbances to certain brain injuries. Studies carried out on victims of head injuries during World War II added further support to these theories. It was in the late 1940s and 1950s that the idea of AD/HD as we now know it began to take theoretical shape. Several studies over this period found a relationship between certain forms of brain defect and distractibility and hyperactivity. By 1972 a Canadian researcher (Douglas) was beginning to describe attention and impulse deficits as characteristic problems. After increasing dissatisfaction with the idea that these symptoms are usually the product of brain damage, Comings (1980) produced a synthesis of research findings from the previous decade that showed compelling evidence compiled in thousands of scientific studies indicating a genetic basis for the condition.

Having described the relatively long pedigree of AD/HD it may seem surprising that it is only very recently that the diagnosis has received popular attention in the UK. The first reason for this is that in the UK, whilst AD/HD has been understood and accepted by a number of medical scientists and psychologists for some time, there has been a preference among practitioners for the World Health Organisation diagnosis of Hyperkinetic Syndrome. As has been suggested earlier, this diagnosis focuses entirely on the symptoms of extreme hyperactivity, which may affect only about half of the children who have AD/HD. This preference has lead clinicians to ignore the form of AD/HD that manifests itself largely in terms of inattentiveness.

It might be argued that whilst the neurological problems that underpin AD/HD (in both its major forms) have been with us for many years, they have been disguised by prevailing social conditions. To put it another way, social factors that exacerbate the symptoms of AD/HD can be seen to have multiplied over recent years. Within school there has been an increasing narrowness of the school curriculum, with its pressure on teachers to move away from child centred teaching strategies, and the concommitant return to an emphasis on testing within a literary medium. The introduction of examination league tables, coupled with LMS and increased emphasis on parental choice has coincided with a dramatic increase in the numbers of children who are permanently excluded from schools.

It has been suggested that these combined factors indicate an increasing lack of tolerance for children's non-conforming behaviour. The demand on schools and teachers to meet stiff attainment targets for all children has placed enormous stress on teachers and pupils. Many teachers believe that the so-called educational reforms of the past decade have placed them and many of their most vulnerable pupils in difficult circumstances, leaving less space within the teaching week to meet children's emotional and other individual needs. Academic pressures which formerly were reserved for children of secondary age are now being introduced into the primary school, at a time of dwindling resources.

Added to these within-school problems are wider social problems, which have been associated (Rutter and Smith, 1995) with an alarming increase in the proportion of young people suffering from psycho-social disorders (such as delinquency, suicidal behaviour, eating disorders, and clinical depression). These outcomes are hypothesised to be associated with a widespread increase in the practical insecurities of childhood, which are in turn associated with problems such as:

● increased youth unemployment
● increased likelihood of family break up
● increased isolation of youth from other age groups, as a result of the development of a powerful youth culture in the western world
● expectation of self determination at increasingly young ages.

Whilst none of the social conditions so far mentioned can be cited as the direct causes of AD/HD, they all represent circumstances that are likely to make life extra difficult for the individual with AD/HD. For example, children with the kinds of attentional and behavioural difficulties associated with AD/HD are likely to have had more opportunities in schools in the past to work at tasks that did not accentuate their weaknesses. There are now fewer opportunities for such 'alternative curricula' which would (by definition) automatically fail the Office for Standards in Education (OFSTED) test (see the OFSTED reports of the first Pupil Referral Units).

Similarly, the emotional and cognitive resources that children with AD/HD might, in ideal conditions, exert to compensate for their neurological deficiencies, are likely to be taken up with dealing with the stresses and strains of living in a world that is characterised by increasing personal and social insecurity.

The key point here is that whilst AD/HD is a problem that has its roots in neurology, it only becomes a problem in certain circumstances. Problems of impulse control, attention and hyperactivity only become problems in circumstances that require control of these faculties to an extent that is beyond the capabilities of the individual.

We each have a stress threshhold which if exceeded leaves us feeling restless and inattentive. For most of the readers of this book this threshhold is (perhaps) breached only occasionally. It is a very rare thing for a teacher or lecturer to have to sit and listen to someone else for sustained periods of time. Teachers and lecturers, by virtue of their roles, tend to be in charge of the agenda that is set within their classes. It is only in staff meetings, or during INSET sessions when they have to submit themselves to others' agendas that teachers tend to experience the kinds of stresses that children with AD/HD find intolerable. To take this point further, we can all probably identify colleagues who find this experience less tolerable than others. We all find our tolerance for such circumstances stretched (sometimes to breaking point) when we have additional stressors to deal with (e.g. a long INSET session on a topic that is not immediately relevant, at a time when one has pressing tasks to deal with). How many of us are able to maintain the impression of interest, diligence, compliance and good personal organisation in such conditions? How many of us for example, fidget, mumble to our neighbours, become distracted by the amusing or trivial, seek diversions, roll our eyes or shuffle our papers, during meetings where we are understimulated? For the child with AD/HD almost every lesson can create the kinds of stresses that we experience occasionally. These problems are further exacerbated by the wider social climate, that is a source of increasing stress for all children and many adults.

Responding effectively to AD/HD

It should be clear to the reader by now that AD/HD is a complex phenomenon. The primary cause of the condition is biological. Children with AD/HD experience the world differently to most other children. The more severely affected they are, the greater the difference between their experience and that of other children. The nature of this different experience is such that these children put enormous stress on people with whom they interact: parents, siblings, fellow pupils and teachers. Thus, whilst it is not accurate to say that the problems associated with AD/HD are the product of poor parenting or inappropriate teaching, it is the case that the kinds of problems presented by children with AD/HD place extreme demands on the skills of parents and teachers. Many of the *secondary* problems associated with AD/HD, such as oppositional behaviour can be avoided or remedied by application of particular handling skills by teachers and parents.

AD/HD, therefore, is *not* simply a biomedical issue. It is a multi-faceted problem, having a bio-medical component, a psychological component and a social component. If we consider an effective response to AD/HD to go beyond mere control of behaviour, by helping to facilitate social integration and access to experiences that enhance emotional and cognitive development, then it is essential that interventions be made that involve biological, psychological and social factors. These matters will be dealt with in detail in forthcoming chapters. Here a brief preview will be given of what such interventions might look like.

Medication is commonly prescribed by physicians to help deal with AD/HD. Contrary to some popular speculation that medication is used to sedate the most commonly prescribed forms of medication are pychostimulants that have the effect of making the person with AD/HD more alert and more able to focus and sustain attention. Medication may often be a necessary condition for successful treatment of AD/HD, but it is rarely a sufficient condition. Medication merely has the effect of enabling the child with AD/HD to benefit from other forms of intervention, many of which fall under the province of the teacher.

Behaviour management strategies, applied in both the home and school are often associated with positive outcomes, when applied in conjuction with appropriate medication. The basic principles of behaviour management (well known to many teachers in the UK and Ireland) involve setting clear behavioural expectations and encouraging the performance of these expectations through the manipulation of circumstances surrounding or following the performance of certain behaviours. Where behaviours are desirable they are rewarded (or 'reinforced'); where they are undesirable they are met with negative reinforcement, that is the denial of reinforcement, through (for example) the use of 'time out' or ignoring strategies.

Educational interventions involve creating circumstances which are most conducive to the learning needs and styles of children with AD/HD. Examples of educational interventions may include catering for different cognitive styles, which for many children with AD/HD can involve allowing them to engage with learning situations through tactile or kinesthetic involvement as opposed to the more conventional auditory or literary styles. Other educational interventions include: an emphasis on clarity and precision in the presentation of learning tasks; care in the sequencing and structuring of learning tasks; involvement of the student in design and monitoring of learning tasks; frequent and prompt feedback to the student on performance; care in the placement of students with AD/HD in relation to other students.

Environmental interventions include minimising gross environmental distractors such as extraneous noise in the classroom, though the practice of stripping the environment of all features that might cause distraction, such as pictures on walls, is probably educationally counterproductive. A boring environment will simply encourage the child with AD/HD to be distracted by his or her own thoughts. What is important here is that the desired focus of the child's attention is more stimulating and interesting than potential distractors. Sensory deprivation is unlikely to be educationally useful! Other important ways of making the environment friendly towards the child with AD/HD involve such things as: making organisational structures, rules and routines simple and easy to follow and recall; minimising opportunities for children to get lost or lose things (e.g. by reducing the frequency of lesson changeovers) and establishing an ethos that stresses tolerance and supports individual differences among children.

Social training is often a vital component of successful work with children with AD/HD. Impulsiveness can make these children very tiresome to their peers and teachers. The rejection and isolation that often follows from this may make the child with AD/HD antisocial. In such circumstances it is necessary to educate the child in some of the basic skills of social interaction. Another important subset of social skills are *self-advocacy skills*. It is important for children not to be made to feel ashamed or guilty for their lapses in concentration, and to have the confidence to (for example) approach the teacher and ask for a point to be restated or the homework task to be repeated/explained one more time.

Cognitive training involves helping the child with AD/HD to develop strategies to learn skills that may compensate for some their cognitive difficulties. A key skill here is the learning of mnemonic strategies to aid recall.

Summary

- AD/HD is a medical diagnosis applied to children and adults who have serious developmental, behavioural and cognitive difficulties when compared with their peers. It manifests itself in terms the individual's difficulties in one or more of the following areas:

    - sustaining attention
    - controlling impulsivity
    - controlling motor activity

There are three main subtypes:

    - mainly inattentive (without hyperactivity)
    - mainly hyperactive
    - combined type

- AD/HD manifests itself in the home and classroom in terms of problems with self control, following rules and organisation.
- The experience of AD/HD, by the sufferer, is often one of bewilderment. They are blamed for what looks like willful misbehaviour or lack of motivation, yet they do not have control over the behaviour that cause the problems. They are often confused because they believe that they are trying as hard as they can — which indeed they often are.
- A secondary effect of AD/HD is that constant blaming and rejection leads to non-compliant behaviour and disaffection. Like most people, the child with AD/HD eventually tires of what he or she see as unfair treatment and rebels.
- AD/HD is believed to be caused by a chronic underfunctioning in the brain chemistry that regulates motor activity, implusivity and attention.

- AD/HD looks like and overlaps with many other problems (including delinquency and learning problems), but is distinct from them.
- Accurate diagnosis of AD/HD depends on lengthy and rigorous assessment procedures.
- Authentic AD/HD is a fairly rare condition, thought to affect about 5 per cent of the population. It is most prevalent in young people, although recent studies show that between 30 per cent and 70 per cent of people carry some or all of the traits into adulthood.
- Effective treatment of AD/HD most often involves a multi-disciplinary approach, including medical, psychological, social and educational interventions. AD/HD is not caused by poor parenting or ineffective teaching. Its effects, however, can be minimised, and in the case of mild forms of AD/HD, neutralised by skilled parenting and teaching.

QUESTIONS

1. How do you react to the concept of AD/HD?
Consider what you have just read in terms of:

   - your personal beliefs
   - the value of the concept of AD/HD to the teacher
   - problems the AD/HD concept might create for the teacher
   - the uses and possible abuses of the AD/HD diagnosis

2. If 5 out every 100 people have the diagnosis:

   - how many students in your school are likely to have it?
   - how many staff are likely to have it?

3. What aspects of your school (and schools in general) would make life difficult for a child with AD/HD?

4. What could be done in your school (and other schools) to assist the child with AD/HD (in ways that are conducive to effective learning for the child with AD/HD and other children)?

CHAPTER 2

How do we know when it is AD/HD and not something else?

Precise, thorough assessment is essential to ensure that children are not mis-diagnosed and that they receive appropriate help. In this chapter, the assessment process is described, with particular reference to the SEN Code of Practice (DFE, 1994) and the roles of various assessment team members. The teacher's role is also highlighted.

First, however, a brief discussion of several issues for consideration prior to initiating or participating in assessment is provided. While these concerns are not exhaustive, they are common to the assessment of AD/HD, and therefore deserve to be highlighted. They are: *the importance of the parent-teacher relationship*, and general concerns of teachers in relation to the AD/HD diagnosis that express *personal attitudes, beliefs and values*.

The parent–teacher relationship in AD/HD assessment

Unfortunately, by the time a child's social and academic difficulties have progressed to the point at which AD/HD is being considered, parents and teachers may have become adversaries. As in any partnership, the teacher-parent relationship, created to help the child, can sometimes be eroded through a cycle of anger, criticism and blame.

This cycle occurs partly because of the nature of AD/HD itself. The condition is complex, 'invisible' in terms of physical signifiers, showing itself through inconsistent symptoms, and, although organic in origin, is experienced primarily socially by observers. It is thus easy for onlookers to assume that the emotional and behavioural difficulties associated with AD/HD must invariably be the product of negative social/family factors, e.g. inept, neglectful or abusive parents, or serious family dysfunction.

Many parents are understandably upset and angry when professionals (physicians, psychologists, social workers, teachers) subtly infer or openly suggest that they have caused their child's AD/HD problems. Blau and Gullota (1996) note that: 'The major family contribution to AD/HD is genetic; AD/HD is considered a heritable disorder. There is no evidence that parenting practices *per se* cause AD/HD, although parents of AD/HD children report considerable stress. . . '

Researchers who have studied the patterns of interaction between parents and children with AD/HD do agree, however, that a negative cycle is often established early in life, as the child's AD/HD behaviours place increasing demands on the parent's emotional and physical resources. Mothers of children with AD/HD sometimes attract chronic blame and criticism from their partners, spouses, parents and immediate family members, for their apparent inability to manage the child's difficult and annoying behaviours.

These mothers are compared with other, more 'successful' mothers in the family or community, and found wanting because their child continues to have problems that other children don't have. They lose confidence and self-esteem, in addition to exhausting their positive emotional reserves to bring to bear on the situation, by striving even harder to control the child's behaviour to somehow 'normalise' him or her. In this process, the mother's own behaviour can become quite critical, authoritarian and demanding as she must repeatedly discipline the child in an effort to solve the problem. This increasing volume of negative inputs over time can lead to further negative consequences for the child, apparently confirming the suspicions of other adult observers that the problems are indeed rooted in 'toxic' mothering practices. Thus, extended family, friends, teachers, and community authorities are often quick to blame mothers because their children do not conform to the social expectations and rules their peers seem to adapt to quite easily over time.

This negative family cycle is often paralleled in the classroom. The parental situation is analogous to that of teachers who are first blamed for the misbehaviour of children, and then criticised for failing to handle or solve the problem successfully. Teachers are caught in the same 'double bind' that parents are, in that they are twice victimised in the situation.

Teachers are people too. Their interactions with children with AD/HD often mirror those of the stressed parents. Teachers, like parents and peers, frequently find they are personally put off by the child's AD/HD characteristics — both socially and academically. Teachers are already stressed by the demands of managing a classroom full of children who have a variety of other needs and problems in addition to those of the child with AD/HD. It can be very difficult for them to find positive ways of interacting with a disruptive, hyperactive child who may also be aggressive, demanding, and intrusive, in addition to being apparently disinterested in education — which the teacher values enough to have made it a career. It can be equally challenging to respond favourably to a withdrawn, non-hyperactive child who appears to be uninterested in classroom life, or unmotivated to perform minimum tasks or to complete homework.

If a child appears bright, yet consistently under-performs in a class, teachers may either blame the child as lazy, or themselves as a failure. Because of their neurological differences, children with AD/HD are not as responsive to behavioural rewards and consequences as other children. Teachers, like parents, sometimes lose patience with the child when repeated, 'tried- and -true' methods of behavioural management that work on others are just not effective in reducing or eliminating unwanted behaviours. Thus a teacher who feel professionally competent, and who refuses to 'blame' the child, will often blame the parents for either failure to properly parent, or sometimes abuse.

The child with AD/HD challenges and disrupts classroom management efforts and systems, just as they can disrupt the system of family life. This child annoys and disturbs teachers as well as peers, which are the nuisance factors that tend to result in these pupils being rejected or neglected by their classmates. The teacher, like the parent, can often enter the assessment process, and the partnership with the partner in a state of anger and frustration. Teachers suffer 'battle fatigue' in much the same way parents do.

When parents and teachers come together to discuss the child's problems, they must be aware that such damaging cycles of interaction may have been in place for many years. The later in the child's life the assessment process occurs, the greater the chances that children, parents and teachers are locked into this difficult cycle. It is critical to acknowledge this possibility, and to refrain from criticising and blaming each other for the problem. The parent-teacher relationship is normally a delicate one, and in the case of AD/HD allowances should be made by both parties that the situation *is no one's fault* — though both parties can do much to address the problem effectively. *It is never too late*, but, if this relationship, that forms the core of the assessment team, is strained, hostile, or adversarial, the entire assessment process suffers — and ultimately the child as well.

Personal beliefs, values and attitudes

Everyone carries with them *beliefs*, *assumptions*, *values* and *attitudes* about what motivates human behaviour, how children are best trained, guided and educated, what course moral development should take, what constitutes good and bad behaviour in children, what distinguishes a 'legitimate' reason for underachievement or failure, from a 'flimsy' excuse, and what constitutes reasonable and effective discipline. These perspectives also shape what 'qualifies', in their view, as a legitimate disability, handicap or impairment and what does not. Often these personal perspectives colour ways in which teachers interact with children, parents and other professionals.

Sometimes, because of the complexity and physical 'invisibility' of AD/HD, it can be difficult for parents and teachers to act effectively in their assessment roles without first identifying, analysing and reconciling their own deeply rooted beliefs, values and attitudes with the diagnosis itself. Obvious physical abnormalities are certainly easier for an observer to accept and address directly, and to make attitudinal adjustments in relation to.

Often, in the presence of AD/HD, apparently 'normal' children, who are intellectually able, yet fail to achieve for reasons not obvious to the eye, are blamed for being 'lazy', 'naughty', or 'slow'. They become victims twice over — first of their disorder, and second of misapplied social disapproval, which erodes self-esteem and motivation over time. This disapproval likely has roots in the observer's personal beliefs, values and attitudes related to such things as the work ethic (industry over 'idleness' or activity for its own sake), respect for authority (obeying elders without challenge), social conformity (co-operation, fitting in with the group), and 'good' manners (culturally preferred social behaviours).

Thus, in order for the assessment activity to be successful, it is vital for all team members to initially (1) reflect on their own personal values, beliefs, attitudes and judgements regarding parents and children in general, (2) identify areas of potential personal or professional bias which may come into conflict with the views and perspectives of other team members, and (3) understand implicitly held perceptions about the nature of self-discipline, behavioural control and restraint — all areas of pervasive impairment in AD/HD .

An overview of assessment

Assessment must include consideration of a wide range of possible contributory factors that will be biological, psychological, social and/or cultural — all of which interact in producing problems and difficulties experienced by the child. Importantly, assessment will also seek to identify the child's 'bio-psycho-social' strengths and abilities. These will ultimately form the basis of the child's progress — hopefully success — in school and in life.

This neurological disorder often shows itself in subtle and inconsistent ways, thus identification and assessment processes are aimed at investigating *long-term emotional and behavioural patterns* displayed by the child in various settings, over an extensive period of time.

Because AD/HD is not effectively assessed by one individual, or through either a simple medical test, or single, brief physical exam, it is imperative that all individuals participating in AD/HD assessment understand first its basic character, in order to fulfil their roles and responsibilities in assessment, diagnosis and intervention.

AD/HD and the (SEN) Code Of Practice (Department for Education, 1994)

Concern over a child's emotional state, social behaviour or academic achievement can originate in the family, community, clinic or school. Although teachers are not always the first to identify pupils at risk for the diagnosis, they are well placed to do so. Because AD/HD traits swiftly come into direct conflict with the demands of schools for pupils to remain physically immobile, focus attention, and stifle impulses for long periods of the day the classroom regularly becomes the first place in which they become problematic. With passing time, AD/HD traits become increasingly obvious when held against the backdrop of schools' social demands and expectations, and developmental benchmarks. The inability (sometimes misread as oppositionality) of the child with AD/HD to conform is a trigger for identification for assessment.

The classroom is thus the crucible in which the expression and identification of AD/HD traits take place, followed by provision of individualised assistance — all leading ideally to transformation of the child's negative experience into one of success. Teachers are ideally placed to initiate the assessment process, contribute to it in substantive ways and to later employ and evaluate social and academic strategies. Through their efforts the child's difficulties are mediated to encourage positive social and scholarly results.

Although historically the value of teachers' contributions may have been overlooked the importance of the their role in relation to assessing and treating this condition cannot be overstated. The framework in which teachers' potential contributions can perhaps best be harnessed is the SEN Code of Practice. It is described in the remainder of this section in general terms in relation to the AD/HD diagnosis.

The Code of Practice presently makes no specific reference to AD/HD as a category of SEN, but uses the general terms: 'a medical condition, disability or developmental delay', which may illicit adult concerns in relation to the child's health. In the context of the Code, then, the specialist knowledge about various difficulties is provided by experts in the consultant role. The Code's principles and procedures are quite consistent with approaches suggested by scholarly and clinical literature on the subject (Barkley, 1990; Goldstein and Goldstein, 1990). Whilst it is not a problem that AD/HD is not specified within the Code of Practice, it *is* important to recognise this as a possible limitation. Teachers and others attempting to gain insight into the child's problems and needs must be informed about the full array of possible interpretations so they do not arrive at inaccurate conclusions, which can perhaps in turn result in possible harm to the child. The Code of Practice is thus a useful vehicle for framing general AD/HD assessment activities when it is used in conjunction with current information specific to the disorder.

Arriving at a precise, appropriate and *correct* AD/HD diagnosis necessarily relies on the objective, systematic collection of both qualitative and quantitative information, from a variety of sources having direct knowledge of the pupil. No single evaluator (parent, teacher, physician, psychologist) possesses the array of information required to unilaterally diagnose. Likewise, an accurate diagnosis cannot, and should not, be taken on the basis of a single incident or interview, standard physical examination, or parental demand. Again, the Code of Practice outlines systematic procedures that if followed will lead to compilation of information necessary to arrive at a decision about whether or not AD/HD is present.

The Code of Practice outlines a five stage model for SEN identification and assessment, stressing that the importance of early identification, assessment and provision 'cannot be over-emphasised'. The rationale for this approach is that early action fosters more effective child response with the least disruption of school organisation and curriculum delivery. It suggests that to assist this process '. . . the school will wish to make use of any appropriate screening or assessment tools which . . . enable the school to consider children's achievements and progress' (C.o.P. p.10).

In addition, it is recommended that schools make full use of information available when pupils transfer between phases, and that they are 'open and responsive to expressions of concern and information provided by parents.' (C.o.P. p.10).

Stage 1 in relation to AD/HD — Concern, identification and initial action

AD/HD is widely thought to be only hyperactivity so many parents and professionals profess to be able to 'spot' one a mile away. Ideas and stereotypes abound in popular and professional culture about the 'wild child,' the child 'terror', the 'hyperactive horror,' and 'the bad seed.' Such lurid and overly dramatic characterisations fuel parents' and teachers' concerns and muddy the waters about what they believe they are identifying. It should be stressed that AD/HD is much more than just physical overactivity, and that all overactivity is not hyperactivity as defined within the AD/HD diagnostic criteria.

Concerns about a child's classroom and/or home functioning may be raised by the parent to the teacher, or vice versa. What aspects of AD/HD might be cause for concern by either party – to trigger stage 1? Perhaps the best way of answering this question is to refer to the APA diagnostic criteria for the disorder. This list of 14 core behaviours forms the basis of the syndrome when certain conditions are met : (1) onset before age seven, (2) persistence of symptoms over six months, (3) measured IQ of over 70, (4) symptoms in more than one setting, e.g. home and school, and (5) absence of pervasive developmental disorders. Mild, moderate and severe degrees are recognised, and it should be noted that a child need only show 8 of the 14 behaviours in order to attract the diagnosis (although many children show more). Teachers should be concerned if a child consistently exhibits the behaviours listed in the diagnostic criteria.

It should be stressed that, taken individually, each behaviour may seem quite 'normal' — and in fact often is. AD/HD is often described as a 'developmental' disorder, because it is defined by chronic problems at the extreme end of the developmental continuum. These difficulties are considered to be 'clinically significant' when the child's behaviour meets the criteria and conditions listed above in *comparison with 'normal' peers*. All children express these behaviours sometimes, particularly in early childhood. However, what should concern a classroom teacher is when the child continues to express a majority of these behaviours chronically, and long after peers have moved on. It is the intensity and chronicity of the behaviours that form the basis for concern.

In very young children (3–6 years) concerns of this nature that might lead eventually to AD/HD assessment and diagnosis should be noted and subjected to careful analysis—*first in terms of natural developmental norms*. Emotional and behavioural patterns in this group can vary greatly among individuals within the range of normal development, which is the reason the AD/HD diagnosis is typically not assigned to children prior to age 7 (although it will depend upon long-term patterns which will have been observed and analysed from infancy by parents and others). It should be remembered, however, that occasionally, extremely hyperactive infants may attract the diagnosis prior to age 7. In such cases, behavioural management tends to be the preferred intervention, although on rare occasions medication will also be used.

Teacher identification of possible AD/HD behaviours rests on concerns generated from repeated closehand observations of, and interactions with, the child displaying difficulties. The keys to sorting episodic social or environmental problems, or disease processes which can mimic AD/HD (pseudo-AD/HD) are to first understand clearly the 14 core behaviours and then to observe carefully and thoughtfully over time to discover the *overall pattern of emotional and behavioural expression*.

AD/HD is in some ways a 'chameleon' disorder. One of its main hallmarks is *inconsistency*. This can confuse and frustrate teachers and others during all stages of assessment. Many things can influence the way in which each individual displays their strengths or difficulties. Stress, health, degree of impairment, social and environmental changes and conditions, diet, and sleep can all affect what an observer sees on any given day.

For example, a pupil whose classroom performance pattern includes classwork marks punctuated by high and low scores, high frequency of incomplete, missing and late written work, chronic handwriting difficulties, and an inexplicable gap between a high level of verbal participation and low quantity of written work — is a likely candidate for further evaluation. Such a pupil may also have drifted into the role of 'class clown' in an effort to preserve declining self-esteem, in order to gain some peer status. This profile is highly suspect when this pupil also seems to be as genuinely confused as the teacher and everyone else about the cause(s) of his or her difficulties. Typical answers to probing questions might be: 'I don't know', 'I didn't understand what I was supposed to do', 'I forgot,' 'I started to do it but didn't finish', 'I left it at home', 'I left it in my desk in my form room', 'I didn't hear the instructions', 'I didn't write it down.'

When all attempts to modify this pupil's behavioural and academic patterns using standard behavioural management and differentiation methods seem to fail, concern — in the formal sense of the Code of Practice — should be shown. Children with AD/HD are less affected by rewards in comparison to peers so pupils displaying AD/HD symptom patterns who also seem to be emotionally 'needy', 'attention seeking' and unsatisfied by token/point schemes that work well with their classmates, may also be in need of closer scrutiny.

In addition to variability of symptom expression, it is also very important to remember that there are two currently recognised subtypes, which may look quite dissimilar in the classroom context: the hyperactive-impulsive and the impulsive-inattentive. The stereotypical AD/HD child mentioned previously — the hyperactive classroom 'terror' — is displaying the most obvious, *but by no means the most important*, symptom of the disorder — from the child's perspective. Although from the teacher's perspective this child's disruptive, oppositional and sometimes aggressive behaviour may seem to be the primary problem in terms of classroom behavioural management, clinically speaking it is more likely that the impulsivity is the more serious of the two in terms of the child's projected improvement and overall success.

The non-hyperactive child's traits are described in Chapter 1. This pupil will likely cause different concerns at Stage 1 than the hyperactive child, but no less serious from the child's perspective. The danger with this type of AD/HD is that teachers may not feel they are observing any emotional or behavioural problems, and thus fail to identify this child until much later than one whose overactivity or aggression is disrupting class. The non-hyperactive child is not just suffering from a mild case of hyperactivity, but from a different, yet related set of problems that can severely impede social and academic success.

Initial teacher concerns will usually centre on the child's sluggishness, day dreaming, chronic failure to complete tasks and homework, disorganisation and inconsistent marks. Often these children do not present a problem to the teacher at all in terms of classroom management, as they are often socially passive, shy, introverted, non-challenging, and compliant. These traits may be mistaken by some teachers as 'good' behaviour, especially in classrooms where docility and passivity are highly valued. Where this view is held, it should be re-examined, as in some cases these children eventually display secondary difficulties such as depression, anxiety and vulnerability to substance abuse or suicidal behaviour, in addition to school failure.

Identifying girls with AD/HD

Stage 1 is critical in relation to girls, primarily because teacher concerns about girls typically come later, if at all, when compared with boys. AD/HD in girls and women has not been well studied, but existing research and expert opinion suggests that girls are underidentified for AD/HD because they typically do not exhibit the symptoms of hyperactivity or aggression that boys do. Girls thus appear to be underdiagnosed, in that they are either overlooked or diagnosed at later ages. Current professional belief therefore holds that girls with AD/HD comprise a substantial underserved group of children.

There are many possible explanations for the historical differences in reported male and female prevalence of AD/HD, although little research exists to verify such hypotheses. They include, but are not limited to the following.

1. Externalising AD/HD behaviours of boys are more socially disruptive, disturbing and threatening than the internalising problems more common in girls.

2. Historically, rigidly defined sex roles structured the family, school and life experiences of males and females very differently (boys were expected to achieve in school and career, girls were not widely educated or expected to achieve in school or career) — thus, academic, emotional and behavioural difficulties of girls were more likely seen as an individual rather than a social problem.

3. A more severe level of biological impairment may be necessary in girls in order to be noticed by observers as cause for concern.

It can be argued that the problems girls present to teachers and parents are perhaps more easily accommodated socially, in that the passivity associated with the non-hyperactive type aligns quite naturally with traditional sex-role expectations, e.g. girls are generally more passive, compliant, less physically aggressive and less overtly challenging to adult authority.

Non-hyperactive females are more likely to be noticed in the classroom because of their chronic academic underachievement, their 'day dreaminess,' and through evidence of specific learning difficulties. Although they can indeed develop oppositional defiant behaviour and conduct disorder like males, they tend to act out these tendencies more covertly, through such anti-social actions as shoplifting and sexual promiscuity, rather than through physical aggression.

In sum, the trigger for Stage 1 is expression of concern about a child in relation to the AD/HD traits if they are known by the teacher. In cases in which teachers may not be familiar with AD/HD, they will still be likely to trigger this stage because, even without that particular label, the AD/HD traits will typically be presenting as problems in the classroom. For this reason the 'Action Plan' described in Chapter 3 can be a useful approach to teachers who are seeking day-to-day, practical strategies to assist the child in either overcoming difficulties, or during the interim period between activating Stage 2.

The purposes of assessment are generally two: first, to identify and eliminate possible causes for the difficulties which are NOT AD/HD, e.g.

psycho-social problems with environmental causes, episodic stress-related difficulties, and/or disease or other medical conditions that are primary in causing symptoms, which, when treated, end the behaviours resembling AD/HD; Secondly, to determine the nature of the child's specific needs, within a context that accounts also for their strengths and abilities. Stage 2 further addresses these purposes.

Stage 2 in relation to AD/HD—Gathering information and offering provision

At this stage 'the SEN co-ordinator takes the lead in assessing the child's learning difficulty, and planning, monitoring and reviewing the special educational provision, working with the child's teachers and ensuring that the child's parents are consulted'.

The SEN co-ordinator, in addition to the classroom teacher, should be informed about the AD/HD diagnosis in order for this set of activities to be accomplished effectively. This includes having (1) general background knowledge of the history and evolving conceptualisations of the condition, (2) general knowledge of current scientific theories of causation, (3) familiarity with signs and symptoms expressed in the diagnostic criteria, (4) knowledge of various related learning difficulties and common co-occurring medical problems, (5) knowledge of biological and social factors that can mimic AD/HD symptoms without being AD/HD, (6) long-term risks and possible outcomes of the disorder, and (7) the multi-modal treatment framework most often recommended for both types of AD/HD.

The SEN co-ordinator must also have thorough knowledge of various methods used to collect information for use in ruling out pseudo-AD/HD, and a cursory knowledge of medical tests used to rule out disease and injury processes which mimic AD/HD, that can be treated to reduce or eliminate symptoms.

Armed with this broad framework of background information, the SENCO then organises the in-school collection of various impressions and perspectives of parents, teachers, peers and siblings for documentation into an assessment file. Ideally, as many people as have pertinent knowledge as possible are polled. This sampling may be formal or informal, depending on local conditions, but information obtained should be written down for use in devising in-school responses, or in later assessment stages if necessary.

On the basis of information gathered, the SENCO decides whether to seek further advice or to draw up an Individual Education Plan (IEP). If AD/HD is suspected, the education plan should include a structured programme of social and academic responses known to be useful with such problems. If the child's problems are resolved as a result of this programme at this stage, it is not likely that true AD/HD is the underlying problem. If the behaviours and other symptoms persist or worsen despite the efforts of the classroom teacher and the SENCO, this may act as a trigger for Stage 3.

Stage 3 in relation to AD/HD — Outside specialist support

At this stage external specialists are called in to consult on the case. The professionals/specialists most likely to have current , detailed knowledge of AD/HD, its assessment and treatment, are:

- specialist support/advisory teachers (e.g. EBD, speech and language disorders, specific learning difficulties, etc.)

- LEA Advisors (SEN, EBD etc.)
- paediatricians
- psychiatrists
- educational psychologists
- clinical psychologists
- neurologists
- qualified psychotherapists (including family therapists).

In addition to these specialists who might be expected to have specific expertise in relation to AD/HD, there are other qualified professionals whose training and experience, either of the specific child or in specific disciplinary approaches, would be useful at Stage 3.

- Educational Welfare Officers
- General Practitioners
- Social Workers
- Probation Officers

A third group of adults who may also have valuable, first hand experience or knowledge of the child's emotional and behavioural patterns over time may include:

- clergy
- youth and community workers
- aunts, uncles, grandparents
- reliable members of the child's community who interact regularly (merchants, librarians).

Information collected in previous stages is combined with expert advice and pertinent insights drawn from other legitimate sources to develop the individual education plan. The IEP is described in detail in Chapter 3. This plan should be structured to ensure cross-curricular and inter-disciplinary approaches, and is implemented and evaluated periodically.

Stage 4 in relation to AD/HD — LEA: Statutory and multi-disciplinary assessments

There is an expectation that most children's special educational needs will be met effectively in the school-based stages (1–3), without the statutory involvement of the local education authority (LEA). This expectation is consistent with American educational practice as well, in which most pupils with AD/HD are expected to receive classroom accommodations to support their individual learning styles and needs within mainstream settings.

However, in a small number of extreme cases (estimated currently between 2–3 per cent of children in the UK) the LEA will need to conduct a statutory assessment of special educational needs. This step is only undertaken if the LEA believes it needs to determine itself the extent of the child's special educational needs by making a statement. Although, statutory assessment will not always lead to a statement. If 3–5 per cent of all children indeed have AD/HD, it is likely that this group will move through Stages 1–3 and then require further assessment at Stage 4, primarily because of the nature of the condition itself.

'Having decided that the statutory assessment must be made, the LEA must seek parental, educational, medical, psychological and social services advice.' Typically, in relation to AD/HD assessment, the following activities would be undertaken if not previously done, or elaborated in order to continue to define an appropriate approach to provision.

1. *Personal, in-depth interviews* usually conducted by a psychiatrist, psychologist or other mental health professional, of the child, parents and teachers (where possible). It can also be helpful, but not mandatory, to interview siblings, classmates and friends, in order to assess psychosocial development, so critical to childhood adjustment. Most experts agree that such interviews are the single most useful tool in AD/HD assessment, because it is through the close observation of long-term patterns of emotional and behavioural expression that the child's essential difficulties are best understood and defined. The overall portrait of the child constructed by pooling information obtained in interviews, when combined with other tools that can rule out pseudo-AD/HD, is the most compelling evidence for confirming the presence of true AD/HD.

2. *Behavioural schedules* of which many have been devised in the UK and USA, are administered to parents and teachers to be used diagnostically by clinicians who will evaluate assessment information when it is collated. The value of the schedules is that they are constructed to obtain objective evidence to balance against the more subjective evidence provided in the interviews. Both are necessary if a well-rounded picture of the child's situation is to be developed.

These schedules, usually administered by an educational psychologist, include:

- Bristol Social Adjustment Guides (BSAG)
    (Stott and Marston, 1971; Stott, 1975) – UK
- Rutter Child Behaviour Scale, B
    (Rutter, 1967; Rutter *et al.*, 1970) – UK
- Gavin and Singleton Behaviour Checklist – UK
    (Gavin and Singleton, 1984)
- Achenbach and Edelbrock (1983) Child Behaviour Checklist
    (Achenbach *et al.*, 1987; Verhulst *et al.*, 1988; Weisz *et al.*, 1989) US – validated for UK use.

These schedules are specifically designed to identify patterns of cognitive, emotional and behavioural traits associated with AD/HD.

3. *Aptitude Testing.* Because the presence of AD/HD and other conditions such as Oppositional Defiant Disorder (ODD) or Conduct Disorder (CD), depression, or specific learning difficulties can affect the way observers evaluate cognitive functioning, it is important in assessing AD/HD to gain an understanding of the child's general cognitive abilities. It is common for this condition to suggest to some parents, teachers and peers that the child is 'stupid', 'lazy', 'thick', 'slow', — and a host of other unflattering and damaging epithets — so it is critical for evidence of the child's actual abilities to be observed and measured.

Most research shows that pupils with AD/HD are of average or above average intelligence. However, their atypical cognitive styles rooted in the AD/HD neurology, which frequently overlap with language-based information processing difficulties, may present to untrained observers as signs of generally lower intellectual ability. This is particularly the case in cultures which place a high value on verbal processing speed, under the debatable assumption that an accelerated rate of verbal processing is in itself an indicator of general intelligence.

Finally, and perhaps most importantly, a hallmark of AD/HD is academic underachievement, which confounds and perplexes observers, in that children with apparently superior intellectual abilities develop ongoing, substantial 'performance gaps' no one understands. Such gaps between general impressions of high aptitude, or measured IQ and substandard day-to-day academic performance, characterised by erratic performance and disorganisation, are as likely indicators of AD/HD as of lower cognitive aptitude. A related concern here is the compound problem that this combination of difficulties is quickly labelled by adults as lack of motivation or an attitude problem, on the basis that inconsistent performance is a matter of deliberate choice – work avoidance, oppositionality. Thus, to many observers, beliefs about the child's cognitive ability and conscientiousness are mixed together inappropriately, resulting in the observers concluding that the child is lazy, disinterested/unmotivated, rebellious/oppositional or intellectually less capable than peers. It is critical to sort these dimensions of the child's actual traits from observers' beliefs and interpretations through objective analysis of aptitude.

4. *Physiological and Neurological Testing.* It is not a simple task to sort out the many physiological, psychological and social dimensions of a child's behaviour. Sometimes hearing or vision problems can mimic some AD/HD symptoms in a child, other times the presence of neurological based specific learning difficulties (dyslexia, dysgraphia, dyscalculia) dramatically affect the child's learning and classroom behaviour. Impaired cognitive processes critical for scholastic success (linear sequencing, sustained task focus, organising, time management and memory, especially short-term memory) are often present in addition to AD/HD in the same child, especially those without hyperactivity. Other medical conditions or disease processes can present as AD/HD, some of which are neurological or psychological in origin. Other neurological conditions may be the primary problem but may also be compounded by the presence of AD/HD (autism, Tourette's syndrome, clinical depression), or may mimic it. Thus, it is critical to eliminate the many factors other than authentic AD/HD which may cause similar symptoms.

5. *Medical Examination.* The child's general health is obviously very important, for various reasons. Many other medical conditions, syndromes and disease processes can produce AD/HD symptoms in an individual. A general assessment of the child's overall health to establish what problem is primary, and which are secondary, is necessary. However, it should be emphasised that AD/HD cannot be correctly assessed by a general medical examination alone. It is simply not possible for a physician to observe the chronic, often subtle and long-term emotional and behavioural patterns of AD/HD in a single consultation in a surgery. AD/HD is best understood as a web of process problems, requiring a long view, rather than a clinical or medical event, such as a cold or broken arm. Most medical school curricula do not prepare general practitioners to assess or diagnose AD/HD, so few

currently have the training or professional experience with the disorder necessary to discover it unaided by the support of other professionals and informed parents.

In summary, relating Stage 4 purposes and processes to AD/HD assessment, is again a multi-modal effort. Additional expert information will be sought to that which has already been compiled. Stage 4 is initiated if it is felt by parents or school staff involved in previous efforts, that the child's needs remain too complex or demanding for adequate treatment at the school level. This assessment effort will be conducted as a precursor to determining whether or not a statement is required.

Stage 5 in relation to AD/HD — LEA: Statement, provide services, monitor services and review services

If, in this stage the statement is created, additional resources and services are provided in the context of the IEP and other action plans in the case, with monitoring of service effectiveness throughout. Components found in this stage will include a description of required provisions, that may specify a particular school or type of school, attention to non-educational provisions such as medical, psychotherapeutic, and social interventions.

Success in every stage of the Code of Practice requires consistent, collaborative effort by those adults in the child's life best positioned to understand that individual, who are also knowledgeable about AD/HD itself. Throughout the assessment process as structured within the framework of the Code, a positive, supportive and co-operative attitude must be maintained. In the following sections, the roles of various involved parties to AD/HD assessment are discussed in detail.

The parents' role in AD/HD assessment

Effective assessment depends on development and maintenance of a close partnership between parents and teachers. Their co-ordinated efforts, undertaken on behalf of the child, and orchestrated carefully with various other professionals and the child, promote precision in diagnosis and encourage success in eventual SEN provision. The Code of Practice is clear on this need: 'children's progress will be diminished if their parents are not seen as partners in the educational process with unique knowledge and information to impart'.

Parents play various roles in AD/HD identification and assessment, including:

1. initiating identification and assessment process through expression of concern;

2. contributing first-hand information about the child's developmental progress from birth through infancy, and

3. providing ongoing feedback to other members of the assessment team as it progresses through the various stages of the process.

Information provided by parents is invaluable to the assessment effort, as they are in the best position to describe the child's early developments, ongoing patterns of mood and behaviour, interactions with siblings and peers, dietary and sleep habits, medical difficulties such as pre-natal and early childhood diseases and injuries, and current perceptions of the nature of the child's problems, as well as views about the child's strengths and abilities.

Whilst it is the case that pseudo-AD/HD can arise in, or be magnified by family life that is disorganised, chaotic, lacking in basic routines and structure as is common in cases of parental substance abuse, mental illness, and criminality, the research is clear that *parents do not cause AD/HD*, which is, in at least 70 per cent of cases, an inherited syndrome of altered brain chemistry that can lead to numerous emotional and behavioural problems.

For these reasons, teachers and other members of the assessment team should make every effort to treat parents and their perceptions with sensitivity and positive regard. Parents should never be made to feel that they are second-class members of the team should they lack education or professional status, nor dismissed or blamed for causing the problem.

Parent information is typically sought using some or all of the following methods.

1. A personal interview, in which the interviewer seeks first-hand perceptions about the child's problems, a detailed family history including similar or related problems among grandparents, parents, siblings, and other members of the extended family, parenting styles, satisfaction/happiness with marital relationship, and medical problems or mental illness existing within the family unit.

2. Direct observation of parent-child interactions, in either the home or a clinical setting, which, although often difficult to obtain for a host of reasons, can provide insight into the nature of the relationships, communication and parenting styles, and the child's behavioural patterns. Because of the logistical difficulties involved in this information gathering method, it is unusual, but it is still regarded as a desirable activity if there is opportunity.

3. Administration of parent questionnaires and behaviour schedules, which employ a variety of written instruments designed to gain detailed data on parental perceptions of the child within the general family context, as well as specifically related to AD/HD traits of inattentiveness, impulsivity and hyperactivity. Other instruments used in dialogue with parents as part of assessment may include social skills inventories, personality and temperament inventories and measures of self-esteem.

4. Parenting style inventories which assess the ways in which parents discipline and instruct children, as well as identifying their expectations for behaviour, also provide constructive feedback to parents in addition to useful information for the team.

The teacher's role in AD/HD assessment

After entry into school, the classroom teacher enters into a relationship with the child which often entails more concentrated interaction over a longer period of the day than is available to parents. The teacher's daily interaction with the child over a school year places that professional in a position to closely observe problems and strengths of the child, in terms of academic and social learning, peer relationships, temperament, and general health. The teacher's observation over a sustained period of time of the child's individual patterns of development and performance across various dimensions in the classroom context and within school culture provides a rich source of information for the assessment team.

In particular, the teacher's academic training and professional experience position him or her well for comparing and contrasting the child's progress with peers — a perspective that parents and other team members may well lack. The consistency of teacher-pupil daily interaction provides proximity and relationship to the child that is not available to the team as a whole, as parents often work outside the home or are dividing time among the child's siblings prior to school entry, and have shorter periods of daily interaction with the child after school entry.

The Code of Practice is specific about the roles and responsibilities of class teachers and form/year tutors in respect of general SEN identification and assessment. At stage 1, the child's teacher:

1. identifies a special educational need;

2. consults the child's parents and the child in the matter of concern;

3. informs the SEN co-ordinator who registers the childs special needs;

4. collects relevant information about the child in consultation with the SEN coordinator;

5. works closely with the child in the classroom through increased differentiation, and

6. monitors and reviews the child's progress.

In the case of AD/HD, the teacher may identify a child's inattentiveness, inability to concentrate, difficulty following directions/rules, or hyperactivity, in that the child is unusually aggressive, intrusive and rejected by peers, over a long period. If the teacher suspects AD/HD, it should be noted in the consultation with parents and the SEN coordinator, and the remaining steps followed as above.

During Stage 2, characterised by the formulation of an Individualised Education Plan (IEP), the teacher works closely with the SEN coordinator who is responsible for coordinating the child's special educational provision. These two professionals are responsible for the application of special instructional support to the child aimed at remediating the problem at the classroom level, without further recourse to outside experts or additional intervention. Parents should be apprised of the child's progress throughout this stage and be invited to provide information and feedback to support the IEP, e.g. supervising homework, practising behavioural strategies similar to those used in class.

In all other stages of assessment, and later in the provision stages through which the child is served educationally, medically and socially, the teacher continues to act as an advocate, observer, reporter and team member.

The doctor's role in AD/HD assessment

It should be emphasised that AD/HD is a *medical* diagnosis which describes a cluster of traits or symptoms found in children and adults. The diagnostic criteria describe chronic developmental difficulties that impair inter-personal, social, academic and economic functioning throughout life when they occur at extreme levels of intensity and duration.

Whilst parents and teachers occupy critical positions of day-to-day interaction with the child, vantage points from which to contribute invaluable information to the assessment process, *neither actually diagnoses the child* as having AD/HD. The role of parents and teachers is to gather information about the child, intervene to remediate problems or assist/ support the child in early stages of problem identification, and to refer the child's case for clinical evaluation by psychologists and physicians should their efforts eventually be deemed ineffective. Psychologists, whilst also contributing specialist expertise, likewise do not diagnose AD/HD. They, like parents and teachers provide information and consultation to the physician.

There are many routes through which physicians may become involved in AD/HD assessment. There are also several medical specialities which are typically drawn upon, including general practice, neurology, psychiatry, and paediatrics. Historically AD/HD has been somewhat obscure and controversial, so it is not yet reasonable to expect that all members of these medical fields be familiar with it, or have expertise in diagnosing or treating it. However, a vast body of medical literature on AD/HD has grown available over the years, and increasing parental demand for assessment and diagnosis appears to be enlarging the pool of UK medics familiar with it.

Ways in which doctors become involved with AD/HD identification and assessment are many, including but not limited to.

1. Physicians familiar with the condition may suspect it in child patients whose parents are not aware of it,

2. Parents who are aware of the condition may suspect a child of having it and present the child to a GP for diagnosis or referral to a specialist, or go directly to a psychiatrist or neurologist,

3. Parents suspecting their child of having AD/HD may go privately to a specialist/consultant requesting assessment or diagnosis,

4. Teachers or SEN co-ordinators may suggest AD/HD to a parent as a possible explanation for their child's learning problems and thus informally initiate an assessment that in effect circumvents a school-originated/based assessment outlined in the Code of Practice,

5. Neighbours or friends of the parents may suggest AD/HD, and refer to specialists formally or informally,

Although the Code of Practice does not specifically mention AD/HD, it does provide guidance in relation to medically based SEN difficulties. 'A child's difficulty at school may be related to a medical condition, disability or developmental delay, which might be first identified by the child's general practitioner, health visitor, therapist, the school health service, community paediatrician or through a teacher's or parent's expression of anxiety about an aspect of the child's health and development' (p.16). Schools are advised that when they first suspect a medical problem they should, with the consent of the child's parents, consult the school doctor or child's GP.

Medical evaluation for AD/HD should incorporate three components:

1. a complete paediatric physical examination

2. thorough clinical (psychological or psychiatric) interviews of the child/adolescent and parents

3. review of completed teacher and parent behaviour rating schedules/ questionnaires.

Barkley (1990) cautions that in the past medical examinations have been '. . .brief, relatively superficial, and as a result often unreliable and invalid for achieving a diagnosis of AD/HD or identifying other comorbid behavioural, psychiatric and educational conditions'.

As previously noted, AD/HD cannot be adequately or accurately diagnosed in a single clinic visit, nor can a proper diagnosis result from only one of the three components mentioned above. Experts advise that if a physician lacks either or both interview data and rating scale results, that diagnosis be withheld until the three components are complete and available for careful analysis. In other words, the subtle and complex aspects of AD/HD must be viewed through a variety of lenses to be recognised for what they are.

Because AD/HD symptoms can be induced by transient, environmental factors (pseudo-AD/HD) and can also be present (comorbid) with a variety of disease states and can also result from brain injury and pre-natal trauma in addition to genetic inheritance, the medical evaluation is critical in terms of sorting various possible biological causes and effects (differential diagnosis). Medical evaluation aims to identify and explore a variety of symptoms and possible causes and co-occurring problems/conditions, and to narrow possible diagnoses through a process of elimination. It should be noted, however, that routine physical examinations by doctors unfamiliar with AD/HD are usually unhelpful in diagnosing the condition.

The presence of AD/HD cannot be verified by a simple blood or urine test, or by routine checks of eyes, ears, noses or throats. Brain scans show promise for the future, but at present the medical examination must be thorough enough to reveal biological features associated with AD/HD. This condition does not lend itself to conventional medical evaluation and treatment in that information required to make a proper diagnosis cannot be obtained through routine lab tests or a simple conversation between doctor and patient. A complex web of information contributed by parents, teachers and others familiar with the child over time is used to reveal patterns characteristic of AD/HD.

Goldstein and Goldstein (1990) note that the role of the physician in AD/HD diagnostic evaluation can be understood in terms of four questions to be answered.

1. Does the child's history or examination suggest the presence of an underlying medically remediable problem contributing to AD/HD symptoms?

2. Are any medical diagnostic tests needed to determine the presence or absence of such an underlying medical problem?

3. What do the physical and neurological exams show?

4. Are there any pre-existing medical problems evident in the child's history or exam results that indicate an increased risk from medical intervention?

In summary, the aims of medical evaluation are: (1) to identify and rule out events, conditions or disease states known to mimic AD/HD or give rise to AD/HD symptoms, and (2) to obtain information about the child shown in research to be associated with AD/HD or highly correlated with it, to combine with other perceptions for eventual decisions about diagnosis.

Summary

The assessment process is the key to proper diagnosis and appropriate help. Children with AD/HD are at risk for a host of lifelong problems which cannot be provided for if assessment is not precise and accurate. Failure to diagnose children who legitimately have AD/HD may place them at further risk, whilst misdiagnosis can also result in serious problems for them and others. Assessment is the means by which the child's needs are properly identified and analysed so that errors of omission or commission are avoided, and appropriate provision is devised.

In this chapter we have looked at the following:

- the importance of establishing and maintaining a positive, co-operative parent-teacher partnership focused on advocating for the child is paramount;
- assessment and eventual provision will be greatly helped if all team members identify and evaluate their own personal beliefs, values , assumptions in relation to children with EBD, the AD/HD diagnosis itself, and their ways of viewing and interacting with other professionals and parents;
- the assessment process itself is 'multi-modal' in that it is not just a simple medical diagnosis, but is a thorough, systematic analysis of problems and difficulties conducted by a team including parents, teachers, and others interested in the child's well being;
- the SEN Code of Practice is a useful framework within which AD/HD assessment can take place, and
- assessment team members play equally valuable roles, which should be undertaken in a co-operative and supportive spirit.

QUESTIONS

1. What beliefs, assumptions, social values and attitudes do you hold that might either support or conflict with your effectiveness as a member of an AD/HD assessment team?

2. What aspects of your school ethos might either help or hinder effective AD/HD assessment?

3. How does informal staff communication contribute positively and negatively to the assessment of pupils needs?

    (a) consider ways in which the positive may be emphasised, in terms of identifying strengths and abilities, as well as deficits

    (b) consider ways in which negative opinions about pupils' abilities or efforts might be diminished in favour of more impartial observation of behaviour

4. How are parents viewed within your school?

    (a) as members of the team with a valuable contribution to make?

    (b) as overly intrusive and demanding of too much time and resources?

5. What strengths or weaknesses might exist between and among various professions in your school or LEA that could affect the assessment of AD/HD (e.g. resources, time, staff, local politics, special interest groups?.

References

American Psychiatric Association. (1994), *Diagnostic and Statistical Manual of Mental Disorders* (DSM -4th Ed.). Washington, D.C.: Author.

Ayers, H., Clarke, D., and Ross, A. (1996). *Assessing Individual Needs: A Practical Approach* (2nd. Ed.). London: David Fulton Publishers.

Barkley, R.A. (1990), *Attention Deficit Hyperactivity Disorder: A Handbook for Diagnosis and Treatment.* New York: The Guilford Press.

Department for Education. (1994), *The Code of Practice on the Identification and Assessment of Special Educational Needs.* Welsh Office: Central Office of Information.

Dykman, R.A. Ackerman, P.T., and Raney, T.J. (1992), *Research Synthesis on Assessment and Characteristics of Children with Attention Deficit Disorder.* Washington D.C.: Division of Innovation and Development, Office of Special Education Programs, Office of Special Education and Rehabilitative Services, US Department of Education (The Chesapeake Institute).

DuPaul, G.J. and Stoner, G. (1994), *ADHD in the Schools: Assessment and Intervention Strategies.* New York: The Guilford Press.

Goldstein, S. (1995), Understanding and assessing ADHD and related educational, behavioural and emotional disorders. In P. Cooper and K. Ideus *Attention Deficit/Hyperactivity Disorder: Educational, Medical and Cultural Issues.* East Sutton, Kent: The Association of Workers for Children with Emotional and Behavioural Difficulties., pp.116–30.

Hinshaw, S.P. (1994), *Attention Deficits and Hyperactivity in Children*. London: Sage.

McKinney, J.D., Montague, M., and Hocutt, A.M. (1992), *Research Synthesis on Assessment and Identification of Attention Deficit Disorder*. Washington D.C.: Division of Innovation and Development, Office of Special Education Programs, Office of Special Education and Rehabilitative Services, US Department of Education (The Chesapeake Institute).

CHAPTER 3

How can we approach AD/HD from the teacher perspective?

After parents, teachers are probably the adults who have the most significant impact on the development of all children. This is especially the case where socially and academically vulnerable children, such as those with AD/HD, are concerned. The way the child is handled in the school; the way the child is responded to by teachers; the opportunities that the child is given to achieve success—all of these things can make the difference between school being a place that helps children with AD/HD overcome or cope with their difficulties or a place that adds to and exacerbates their difficulties. In this chapter we look at the ways in which teachers can begin to approach the issue of AD/HD in the classroom, and how they can work with students and parents to identify and begin to address the child's needs in positive educational terms.

Working with the AD/HD diagnosis

Remember, there are no 'AD/HD children'; there are only children with AD/HD. AD/HD does not signal that the bearer of the diagnosis is a congenital deviant or criminal. Neither is AD/HD a glamorous or desirable condition that excuses the individual from conforming to the rules that govern the lives of all the rest of us. AD/HD *is a* potentially highly debilitating condition that can lead to disasterous personal and social outcomes when mishandled or misunderstood.

A major task for teachers confronted by AD/HD for the first time is to figure out their own feelings and reactions towards the condition. If AD/HD is perceived to be a bogus condition—an unwelcome import from the land of fast food and 'Coca Cola'—coined to protect incompetent parents from the consequences of their own inadequacies, this may create difficulties. This attitude may have unfortunate consequences for the child who comes into your school bearing the AD/HD diagnosis.

The pragmatic option

In some cases, if teachers focus on their beliefs about the diagnosis, they are in danger of getting off on the wrong foot with the parent(s) and probably the child, by immediately having a conflict of views. A simple way round this problem is to take the the pragmatic option. Whatever the teacher's personal thoughts about the condition, if AD/HD is seen by the parents and child as offering a framework to address to school difficulties, it is at least an opportunity to establish a cooperative relationship with parent and child, which begins with the view that 'now we have identified the root cause of the problem(s) we can use this as a basis to develop ways of meeting our shared objective, which is to solve these problems'.

Talk with the child and parents

Whilst it is important to avoid pathologising the child by focusing to an undue extent on the fact that the child bears the AD/HD diagnosis, it is also important to acknowledge its presence and be prepared to address issues and concerns that relate to it. It is important that parents, teacher and child have a shared understanding of the condition as it affects the child's school performance.

For this understanding to be helpful, it should be based on the principle that the diagnosis is not to be used as an excuse for explaining why the child **cannot** do certain things, but rather should be seen as a source of information which can be used to help the child *overcome* difficulties. Where problems do arise, dialogue should be initiated which has the purpose of defining an appropriate solution, rather than seeking an explanation for the problem or apportioning blame.

A concrete strategy here is to always (as far as possible) link *understanding* of difficulties with a *planned solution* and the clear *expectation* of what is to be achieved by the proposed solution. The focus should always be on creating a clear picture of what the situation will look like when the problem has been dealt with.

For example, whilst it is common for a child with AD/HD to have problems with producing homework on time because the child often misses the homework instructions, it is possible to establish a checking procedure, whereby the teacher or pupil, at the end of each lesson, seeks clarification that the homework has been recorded in an appropriate form. The immediate expectations attached to this planned intervention are:

- that the checking procedure will take place at the appointed times;
- that the child will leave each lesson with a clear record of the homework task (agreed by the teacher);
- that the frequency of homework delivery by the child will improve.

It is important for teachers to be responsive and empathic towards the concerns and difficulties that the child with AD/HD presents, whilst, at the same time, avoiding overprotectiveness or sentimentality. Teachers can help the child with AD/HD and extend their own understanding of the condition by simply *listening* in an accepting and non-judgmental way to the child's account of how it feels and how it affects his or her school performance. (It is equally important, however, to avoid 'leading the witness', by communicating to the child how one expects him or her to feel. This can have the result of creating a self fulfilling prophecy, or simply not giving you access to the information you want). An important effect of this process can be the development of a positive relationship between the teacher and child that will pay enormous dividends at times of stress, when extreme effort is required to persevere with finding solutions to problems and making them work. This is particularly important when we consider the secondary social effects of the condition. Children with AD/HD often have histories of social neglect and rejection which leave them with very fragile egos and poor self-esteem. They (and their families) are often in great need of simple understanding and acceptance of the fact that they are labouring under a difficulty that is not of their own making. Teachers can play a vital role in communicating their acceptance to the children, and, where appropriate, the parents too.

The way in which the teacher behaves towards any child often influences the ways in which other children behave towards that child. It important, therefore, for teachers to be conscious that they are *modelling* the kinds of behaviours that they would like other children to adopt towards the child. Patience and tolerance are very important in this regard.

Of course, teachers also need understanding and acceptance. An important place for acceptance to be shown is in the staffroom. It should be recognised that having a child or children with AD/HD in one's class stretches the skills of the most competent teacher. As noted earlier, however, acceptance and understanding of the condition does not imply that it should be taken as an excuse for not trying or blaming the problem on factors outside the teacher's control. Acceptance and understanding must always be linked with positive expectations and objectives.

The AD/HD Action Plan

Although there is no formal provision for a co-ordinated action plan, we suggest that if the work of the different professionals involved in the assessment and treatment of the condition is to be sucessful, it is important that such a plan exists. The purpose of the plan is to provide the parent(s) and child with a complete overview of the various assessment records and intervention plans. It should also be a point of reference to all the professionals involved, each of whose inputs (e.g. in the form of the medical treatment plan, or IEP) should be made with some understanding of the input of other professionals. The parent is most likely to be the holder of the overall plan.

The Action Plan provides the framework on which the response to AD/HD is based. These plans grow out of the assessment procedures outlined in Chapter 2. The main components of the plan will include:

- a clear account of the child's difficulties
- the precise interventions and provision required to deal with these difficulties
- the roles of the various people involved in the treatment (i.e. parents, the child, professionals such as teachers, doctors, psychologists and social workers)
- clear criteria for evaluating the success of interventions
- a precise statement of the time scale over which the plan is to operate, with details of monitoring and review procedures.

The overall Action Plan may include many different subplans, depending on the outcome of the assessment process. There may be a medical plan, which involves the prescription of medication or a diet plan. There may be a need for psychological intervention in the form of counselling, family therapy, social and parent skills training, which will require the involvement of a psychiatrist, psychologist or social worker. There will almost certainly be a need for an educational plan, the responsibility for which will lie with educational professionals.

The complexity of the condition is such that different cases may involve very different groups of professionals. In these circumstances it may well fall to the parents to act as mediators of and coordinators between the different professionals. Obviously, sometimes this will be a very good situation: the parent(s) will take a proactive role which will empower them and ensure that the intervention process is driven by the needs of the child. Sometimes, however, this will not be the case. For some reason, the parent(s) may not be willing or able to perform this function adequately. In these circumstances it may well fall to one of the professionals involved to maintain an overview: to, in effect, become the informal 'case manager'. The teacher is likely to be one of the best placed people to perform this function, since he or she is likely to have most contact with the child, and may be in a position to see the parent(s) at shorter notice and with greater frequency than other professionals.

This *informal* coordinating role is largely concerned with:

● having an awareness of all of the different measures that are in process and ensuring that the parent(s) and child share this awareness;
● liaising with the parent and child to see how well the programme is working for them;
● to provide support for the parent(s) in helping them make sense of the overall programme, and helping them to deal with concerns and queries they may have (e.g. suggesting when it may be appropriate to approach one of the other professionals involved for further consultation or clarification of a particular issue).

Obviously, if the child has received or is undergoing statutory assessment for SEN under the terms of the *Code of Practice on the Identification and Assessment of Special Educational Needs* (DFE, 1994) this role will be taken formally by the LEA through the *named LEA Officer* and the independent *Named Person*.

Constructing an effective IEP

Under the Code of Practice for SEN (Department for Education, 1994), this educational component will take the form of an Individual Education Plan (IEP). The IEP has a formal status and structure within the terms of the Code of Practice, which only comes into effect when Stage 2 of the Code of Practice has been reached (i.e. when a concern is expressed that a child has Special Educational Needs that require the input of the SEN Coordinator). We suggest, however, that an IEP can serve a useful purpose in precluding the need to move to Stage 2, in some cases, and can be a useful tool for the individual class teacher at Stage 1 of the Code of Practice.

The content of the formal IEP, under the Code of Practice advice, should be:

1. an account of the child's learning difficulties

2. statement of the action required to deal with these difficulies in terms of educational provision

- staff involved frequency of support
- specific programmes/activities/materials/equipment
3. help required from parent at home
4. targets to be achieved within a specified time scale
5. statement of pastoral care or medical requirements
6. monitoring and assessment arrangments
7. review arrangements and dates.

We would argue that before Stage 2 is reached the class teacher would be well advised to adapt certain elements of the formal IEP to their own planning in their attempt to deal with initial difficulties, in the preparation of a 'Stage 1 IEP', the nature of which is described below.

Stage 1 IEP

The Stage 1 IEP is not a requirement of the Code of Practice, and, as such, does not have the formal status of the Stage 2 IEP which is a requirement of the Code. The Stage 1 IEP simply borrows certain elements from the IEP advice in the Code of Practice, and is seen as an *informal document* that supplies a framework for conceptualising and planning a child's individual needs. The document is prepared by the class teacher in consultation with the child and his or her parents.

The components of the Stage 1 IEP are as follows.

1. **An account of the child's learning difficulties.** Record an account of the problems that the child appears to be exhibiting. Be specific. Record actual events in **behavioural** terms (i.e. write down what you have observed happening, not what you **felt** happened).

    State the effects of this behaviour on (a) the child's educational progress; (b) the learning environment for other children.

    Record what you can about the child's own perspective on these problems (interview the child directly if necessary). It is important not to do this in the context of a disciplinary act: that is, do not ask for the child's perspective in the context of an explanation for undesirable behaviour when you are giving a reprimand. This will at best produce a defensive answer and maybe even an oppositional one.

    Provide a statement of what you would consider to be the effect of solving these problems (i.e. what will the situation look like when these problems are solved, in terms of (i) the child's behaviour and learning; (ii) the learning environment for other children).

2. **Statement of the action required** to deal with these problems in terms of:

    - the nature of the support you intend to give the child (e.g. interpersonal; arrangements for individual consultation), staff involved, frequency of support
    - specific interventions/programmes/activities materials/equipment you intend to use (e.g. adjustments to environment/behaviour management strategies/ pairing the child with another child for certain activities).

3. **Parents should be kept informed** of what is going on and consulted in the same way that all parents should be routinely informed and consulted about their child' s status and progress in school. The emphasis at this stage should be placed on the fact that the problems are being dealt with

within the framework of everyday classroom teaching. It is generally seen as good practice for teachers to inform all parents of ways in which they can support their children's educational development and progress by focusing on specific individual needs. At this stage parental consultation should be carried out within this routine framework.

4. **Targets to be achieved within a specified time scale.** What do you intend to achieve, and by when (e.g. to reduce the frequency of specific undesirable behaviours; to increase the frequency of specific desirable behaviours — social and educational, by the end of the current term).

5. **Monitoring and assessment** arrangements. How you are going to measure the extent to which the targets above have been achieved (e.g. procedures for calculating the frequency of desirable and undesirable behaviours).

6. **Review** arrangements and dates. Precise details of when you intend to review and, if necessary, modify the plan.

The Stage 1 IEP should be seen primarily as an informal document. It is a record of agreement about (1) the nature of a set of problems, and (2) a plan of action for dealing with the problems. The main parties to the agreement are the teacher(s) and the pupil. In establishing this plan, the following key principles need to be observed:

- The plan should be produced *collaboratively*, with the child being consulted at every stage of the process of identifying the problems and in devising solutions.
- Problems should be defined as far as possible in *positive* terms, so that the focus is on *solutions* that serve the social and *educational interests* of the child and his or her peers, rather than focusing on what is NOT wanted.
- Solutions should be sought from any available source, with equal attention given to the way in which the environment can be changed to help the child, as well as ways in which the child can be helped to change aspects of him- or herself.
- The needs of the individual and the needs of other children can often be met simultaneously without compromising the quality of experience for either. The close relationship between social and cognitive development can mean that the interests of the child with AD/HD can often be served through pairing the child with other individuals, who in turn will benefit from the experience. An important principle of inclusive education is that all children benefit from the experience of dealing with people who have a variety of different needs.

Ideally the Stage 1 IEP will form the basis for interventions that will enable the child to access the curriculum without the need for further intervention. However, there is clearly a limit to the amount that a classroom teacher can achieve when presented with a child exhibiting extreme difficulties of a type sometimes associated with AD/HD. If after the adminsitration of a Stage 1 IEP, severe problems persist, then the existing groundwork that has gone into the IEP will serve as invaluable *evidence* on which to proceed with the Stage 2 process.

Stage 2 IEP

The Stage 2 IEP is a formal elaboration of the Stage 1 IEP. The classroom teacher's role remains the same as in Stage 1:

- to provide evidence from their own perceptions of the nature of problems and possible solutions (based on rigorous behavioural observation)
- to maintain a positive dialogue with the pupil about these issues
- to meet the child's educational needs as effectively as possible
- to keep the pupil informed of developments in relation to the area of concern (both positive and negative).

It is at this stage, however, that the SEN Co-ordinator (SENCo) becomes directly involved. At this point the IEP becomes a formal requirement. Evidence is now required under the following categories.

Assessment

The nature of the child's difficulties and the evidence on which this is based. This will include

- the *source* of the evidence presented, e.g.:
    - evidence from the teachers informal and formal observations;
    - evidence from the use of rating scales and schedules (see Chapter 2 for details)
    - evidence from student's self-monitoring form;
    - evidence from other specified sources (e.g. medical evidence)
    - the people and professions involved in the assessment (this must include evidence from the parents and the child)

- a *description* of the difficulties
- an account of the likely *underlying* difficulties, that lead to or exacerbate the problem(s), e.g:
    - medical problems (i.e. the AD/HD diagnosis)
    - learning styles
    - teaching styles
    - learning difficulties
    - teaching materials
    - teaching methods
    - organisational factors in the school
    - classroom management techniques
    - student motivation
    - level of student's social skills
    - family background factors
    - peer group influences

Intervention

- *Intervention targets* and *strategies*

(i.e. what are the required outcomes of successful intervention with these problems in educational terms?)
Targets should be stated in terms that are clear and that lend themselves to evalauation. They should also be stated in *positive* and *educational* terms. Thus, for example, a child's AD/HD may manifest itself in hyperactivity that

leads to his or her being out of their seat and interfering with others' work and his or her own progress. The aim of intervention should be seen as not just to *stop* the child from behaving in these ways, but to do so in ways that are beneficial to his or her's and others' educational progress. In this case therefore, appropriate targets might be:

- to increase the amount of time that the child stays on task in his or her seat when this is required
- to improve the quality of the child's interaction with peers in the classroom through showing an awareness of the needs of others
- to increase the amount of positive attention received from peers and staff
- to provide additional support in terms of basic literacy skills.

● *Intervention strategies* (i.e. what is going to be done to solve these problems in terms of class teacher action; involvement of personnel other than the class teacher; specific programmes for the student in the form of training, monitoring, reinforcement and time-out; educational adaptations to meet the student's learning/cognitive specialisations.)

Strategies need to be *realistic*, in that they should consider availability of resources, as well as practical limitations, such as time and expertise. They should be clearly related to the targets set. They should also take careful account of other professional (e.g. medical) advice. For example, a medical report may indicate that a central problem for the child is hyperactivity. As a result medication may be prescribed which is intended to help the child to control this problem. If the child has only recently received the diagnosis it is likely that he or she will have developed habits of behaviour that the medication alone is unlikely to solve. The child will need direct training in *desirable* behaviour. Furthermore, the medication is likely to be more effective at certain times of the day than others, thus highlighting times when the child is likely to be most receptive to educational inputs.

In relation to the above targets, strategies might include:

● teachers using an ignore-rules-praise strategy with the child, particularly in relation to social behaviour, whereby rule breaking behaviour is ignored, and rule compliant behaviour is praised (not only for the target child but for others too, so that positive modelling is also employed);
● providing the child with legitimate opportunities to leave his or her seat under teacher direction;
● direct training in the skills of positive interaction (e.g. gaining attention politely; turn taking in conversation), through direct instruction and modelling;
● use of short-term, time-out procedure when the child's behaviour is unduly disruptive;
● four hours of a Learning Support Assistant time per week; to support the child during seat work and other activities; to carry out and reinforce the social skills training aspect of the programme; to monitor the extent to which the programme is being implemented; and to monitor the child's perceptions of the process, and
● parents to use the planned ignoring-praise strategy; to support the social skills training programme; to use short-term time out procedure; to ensure that the child has an appropriate setting in which to do homework; to be available to offer specific help with homework.

Evaluation

Evaluation methods and an *Evaluation schedule* should be set up which offer a clear and precise means of establishing the success of the interventions in direct relation to the targets set, and within a clear time frame. For example, in relation to the targets and interventions stated above:

Week 1 of schedule:
Take baseline measures of frequency of child's out of seat behaviour in selected lessons and duration of in seat behaviour during periods where in seat behaviour is required. Take account of the effects of medication on the child's receptiveness.

Take baseline measures of the frequency of positive praise statements and negative sanction statements directed at the child.

Describe the nature and frequency of the child's interactions with peers in relation to the positive social skills described in the intervention plan.

Weeks 2 to 6
Implement strategies.

Week 7
Repeat measures carried out in week and compare.
Modify programme as required.

The exact format of the IEP will vary from school to school/ LEA to LEA. It is essential however, that the above elements be covered in an IEP, regardless of the format.

For an IEP to be useful it is essential that:

- it be the product of a collaborative effort between teachers, parents and the child;
- its contents be clearly understood by all involved;
- all involved understand their own roles and those of others in the plan, and
- it be constructed with careful reference to other professional advice (e.g. medical).

Summary

- There are no AD/HD children : only children with AD/HD.
- Knowledge of AD/HD provides a basis for doing something positive, not an excuse for giving up. Understanding of problems should always be linked to expectations and concrete plans for action.
- Effective intervention depends on cooperation between teachers, students and parents, and often the involvement of other professionals.
- The IEP provides a good model for planning a response to AD/HD at all Code of Practice Stages.
- Interventions used by teachers should always be directed at securing positive educational outcomes for the child, rather than simply preventing unwanted behaviour.
- Intervention should be designed in terms of clear targets, definite strategies and have an evaluation component.

Questions

1. What systems are in place in your school to support the teacher who is dealing with a cause for concern at stage 1 of the Code of Practice?

2. What systems are in place in your school for preventing learning and behavioural difficulties from becoming problems? What improvements, if any, could be made here?

3. What routine systems are in place in your school for the review and evaluation of teaching methods? What improvements, if any, could be made here?

4. What is the quality of communication between staff and students like in your school? How do you react to the idea that you should negotiate with and consult with pupils?

5. What are staff-parent relations like in your school? Could they be improved? If so how?

Reference

Department of Education (1994), *Code of Practice on the Identification and Assessment of Special Educational Needs*, London, Department of Education.

CHAPTER 4

Effective teaching for children with AD/HD: How does it look?

In this chapter we consider some of the things that teachers and schools can do to help children with AD/HD to experience school as rewarding and enriching in social, educational and personal terms. The ideas presented here are by no means exhaustive; they are intended to give an insight into the kinds of things that seem to work for teachers of students with AD/HD in mainstream settings.

The chapter is underpinned by the assumption that teaching involves the teacher acting as a mediator between the learning environment/task and the child. It is suggested that in order for this process to be *effective*, it is necessary for the teacher to create circumstances in the learning environment, that enable all children to engage in learning activities in ways that make optimum use of their strengths as learners, and whilst de-emphasising their weaknesses. Where children have serious learning difficulties, mastery of skills to overcome these difficulties becomes an important part of the curriculum.

Working in the context of the National Curriculum

Clearly, the National Curriculum (NC) poses some awkward problems in relation to the education of children with Special Educational Needs, and the needs of children with conditions like AD/HD in particular. The NC assumes that children develop in a fairly linear manner, building skill upon skill and advancing through roughly age related stages with parity across a wide range of school subjects. Many children with AD/HD tend to perform erratically in academic terms: one day they appear to know nothing; to be completely lost and incapable of doing anything right. Another day they may perform to outstanding effect. What they appear to show mastery of on one occasion, however, cannot be relied upon to be repeated on a future occasion. Furthermore, the increasing emphasis of the NC, through the application of timed Standard Assessment Tasks, on children's ability to express their knowledge and understanding of subjects in written answers under time limited examination conditions creates special problems for children with AD/HD. They often take longer to complete tasks than their peers, lose track of time, find it difficult to organise themselves or become confused and lost amid complex sequences of written instructions. They often have difficulty with auditory discrimination, which means they may have difficulty following spoken instructions or tasks (such as those employed in modern languages lessons). Commonly, they have difficulties with written language: both reading and writing.

In spite of such problems these children are often capable of conveying to their teachers a high level of academic understanding and ability. It is this disparity between apparent ability and performance that can be frustrating and confusing for both the teacher and student. However, children with AD/HD often learn well in active situations, such as those involving drama or role play, or where they have the opportunity to engage with learning matter through tactile or kinaesthetic means. Whilst this might be taken to suggest that children with AD/HD are likely to have a greater affinity for certain school subjects (such as creative and expressive arts), it should also be taken to point to the fact that their access to any subject matter will be eased if it is presented through teaching methods that draw on these forms. For example, role play exercises can be used in ALL curriculum subjects.

The child with AD/HD presents often as a child with average to high ability, but with learning difficulties and problems of organisation and behaviour. This poses the teacher a number of key tasks:

- to help to stretch the child cognitively using the child's existing strengths and preferred ways of learning;
- to help the child to catch up on basic skills without making the child feel that his or her lack of these skills makes him or her a failure: whilst the child's cognitive development may not depend on literacy and other formal academic abilities, his or her accumulation of credentials and progress in the NC will;
- to preserve and preferably boost the child's self-esteem, to avoid the descent into disaffection and poor motivation (where such a descent has already occurred, this also needs to be addressed);
- to help the child become socially integrated and not a disruptive influence in the classroom to the detriment of other children, and
- to meet the needs of the child with AD/HD without compromising the experience of other children in the class or school.

Dealing with problems: Some principles

Many of the classroom problems associated with AD/HD present themselves in the form of behavioural problems. These problems will sometimes look *like* laziness or lack of motivation (in the sense that the child appears not to care, to be uninterested, or wilfully unco-operative). Like everyone else, children with AD/HD are sometimes lazy and unwilling to work. Quite a lot of the time, however, for the child with AD/HD what looks like laziness or unwillingness to work is a result of the AD/HD. This means that it is not a problem that will be solved by the child simply trying harder. In these circumstances the child will have to be helped to learn *how* to behave in the desired way.

The aim of intervention with the child with AD/HD, then, is not simply to control or extinguish the unwanted behaviour, it is to help the child develop habits and patterns of behaviour that are socially effective and educationally appropriate.

A valuable way of thinking about behavioural problems is to see them as one or more of five possible types:

- as resulting from the desire to avoid something;
- as resulting from the desire for attention at inappropriate times and in inappropriate ways;
- as resulting from a misunderstanding, communication difficulty, lack of knowledge or information;
- as an involuntary reaction that has a psychological or physiological cause, and or
- resulting from a lack of agreed or shared values.

On the basis of this typology interventions are designed for the child with AD/HD that attempt to:

Remove reasons why a child might wish to avoid positive engagement in lessons

Children with social, learning and emotional difficulties often avoid engagement in lessons not as a *direct* result of their *primary difficulty* but as a *secondary* response based on experiences of humiliation and failure. The object of intervention that follows from this principle is to seek ways of making student involvement as rewarding as possible rather than punishing or otherwise aversive. A rewarding aspect of schooling for most students is the enjoyment of positive relationships with peers and staff. Staff can play a leading role in this process by initiating positive interactions with students, through *warmth, friendliness, humour and the showing of empathy and unconditional positive regard*. In this way teacher behaviour can help to shape a positive atmosphere in which pupils will imitate the teacher model. A very important issue here is that of *blame*. If a teacher is in the habit of emphasising the source of problems and apportioning blame when things go wrong, then obviously children with difficulties are going to receive a lot of negative feedback. A way around this is to adopt a *solution* focus, rather than a problem focus: to ask: what can we do to solve this problem? rather then what is the cause of this problem?

Create circumstances in which positive attention is available for legitimate reasons

Any attention is better than no attention at all. Children with learning and behavioural difficulties sometimes learn that it is easier to get noticed by behaving in negative or foolish ways, than by being a 'good student'. The best thing for teachers to do in these circumstances is to minimise the amount of attention given for negative behaviour and to maximise the amount of attention given for desirable and positive behaviour. It is often the case, for example, that teachers will give positive attention for good academic performance, whilst tending to notice only that social behaviour that is negative. This means that children with learning and behavioural difficulties get plenty of negative attention, and can become alienated as a result. A way to combat this is, to use a well-known phrase 'catch them being good', by drawing attention to and praising positive social behaviour when it occurs whilst ignoring negative behaviour.

Clearly, it is not always possible to ignore negative behaviour. When this happens, the behaviour should be dealt with as unobtrusively as possible, immediately and decisively, such as through the use of time out (i.e. the withdrawal of positive attention). When punishments of this kind are used they should always be accompanied by a clear statement of the reasons why the punishment is necessary and a statement of what the desirable alternative behaviour looks like.

Ensure clear and effective channels of communication.

Key issues here are:

  – clarity of communication
  – willingness to listen
  – willingness to repeat or paraphrase information and/or instructions as often as it takes, without displaying anger or exasperation

Misunderstandings and confrontation can often be avoided when teacher expectations are clearly stated, and children feel empowered to express their concerns or desire for clarification. Similarly, children are far more likely to accept that they have been wrong, if they are given the opportunity to explain their side of the story. Sometimes, of course, their side of the story indicates that they have not been wrong at all.

Be aware of individual differences

It is invaluable for the teacher to have an awareness of the specific circumstances in which individual children perform best. This gives the teacher knowledge of what to expect in certain situations. For example, children with AD/HD can often become overwhelmed by the massive overstimulation they experience in a group situation. This problem, coupled with the poor social skills that are associated with hyperactivity, can lead to disruption and mayhem. If a teacher wishes to avoid this, it might be advisable to place the child with AD/HD in a pair situation, rather than a group. On the other hand, the importance of developing group work skills should not be ignored. If the child with AD/HD is to learn group work skills it may be necessary for the teacher to structure his or her group work experiences with particular care, by, for example, ensuring that the child with AD/HD is placed in a group with children who are skilled in collaboration and cooperation, and thus unlikely to place undue strain on the child's impaired attentional faculties.

Furthermore, in a multicultural society there are many opportunities for conflict between teachers and students that could be avoided by the creation of opportunities for teachers and students (and the wider community) to explore different values and attitudes and the ways these might be accommodated in the classroom so as to avoid conflict.

Effective classroom teaching for children with AD/HD

What follows is a list of practical suggestions that are intended to help the teacher make learning tasks accessible to the child with AD/HD. Many of these points are appropriate to all children, but they are all especially helpful to the child with AD/HD. The key underlying principles are as follows:

1. The need for precision and clarity in communicating with the child with AD/HD so that whatever it is you want the child to do is always sharply

in focus, and not lost in a fog of extraneous detail or ambiguity.

2. The need to protect the child from distraction by (a) reducing unwanted stimuli, (b) increasing desired stimuli and (c) teaching to the child's cognitive and personal strengths.

3. The need to protect and nurture the child's sense of self esteem by (a) maximising opportunities for success, (b) communicating personal warmth and acceptance and (c) through positive recognition in the form of praise and rewards.

The following are some of the approaches that have been found to be successful with children with AD/HD:

- Children with AD/HD are *often hypersensitive to distraction*. It is, therefore, important to ensure that they are seated in the classroom in a place that is (1) relatively free from distraction (away from doors and windows; (2) in a place where the teacher can readily detect if the child is or is not attending, and, if necessary, *intervene without embarrassing the child or disrupting the lesson*. It is also important that a value be placed on calmness and quietness, when appropriate. This is not the same as saying that a quiet classroom is always a good classroom. There are times, however, when the effectiveness of the teaching and learning processes going on in the classroom depends on an atmosphere of quietness and calmness (i.e. when intense individual concentration is required). When this happens the teacher should make efforts to provide it.

- Sometimes the child with AD/HD may have a *greater need for quietness* than other children, because of attention problems. When this happens it is helpful to have a designated quiet place where the child can go.

- Children with AD/HD can also be distracted by their own thoughts, therefore, it is important to ensure that they are stimulated by the required task: *sensory deprivation is not conducive to effective learning*.

- Children with AD/HD benefit from *concise, clear instructions* with as few subparts as possible. They should be encouraged to repeat orally task requirements back to the teacher, preferably in their own words.

- *All* children, and particularly those with AD/HD, benefit from clear, *predictable, uncomplicated routine and structure*. It helps if the day is divided into broad units of time, and that this pattern is repeated daily. Within each block of lesson time there should be a similar breaking down of tasks and activities into a few subtasks/activities. Presenting the child with an enormously detailed list of tasks and subtasks should be avoided. An important goal should be to create a simple overarching daily routine that the child will eventually learn by heart. The number of tasks should be kept small and tight deadlines should be avoided. Complexities of timetabling and working structures merely confuse children with AD/HD, because a major difficulty that goes with this condition is the inability to differentiate between and organise different bits of information. This clearly makes the formal curriculum difficult enough to manage, without having to struggle with the organisational arrangements which surround the curriculum. Once a workable daily timetable has been established this should be publicly displayed and/or taped to the child's desk or inside the child's homework diary.

- *Avoid repetitive tasks.* Whilst the general daily routine should be simple and broadly predictable, the educational content should be as varied and stimulating as possible. If tasks are not stimulating they will allow the child to become easily distracted.
- *Tasks should be broken down* into a small number of short steps. Again, the emphasis should be on reducing complexity and maximising clarity of focus so that the child and the teacher are both clear about what is expected.
- Clearly, the child with AD/HD should be encouraged to tackle tasks of increasing complexity. Initially, however, *tasks should be relatively short.* The length and complexity of tasks should increase only when the pupil has shown success with shorter assignments. This is not only important from the viewpoint of skill development, it is also a valuable way of enhancing the child's self confidence and self-esteem.
- Academic products and performance (e.g. work completion) are nearly always preferred targets for intervention, rather than specific behaviours (e.g. remaining in seat). This stresses the need to *focus on positive,* desirable outcomes rather than the negative, unwanted behaviour.
- Use the DuPaul and Stoner's (1994) 'deadman' test. If a dead person can carry out the behaviour you require, it is not behaviour. Negative expectations of this kind are likely to be problematic for all children Behavioural *requirements should involve positive behaviours*, rather than the absence of behaviour (if the pupils are alive that is).
- Children with AD/HD *often require more specific and more frequent feedback* on their work performance than most pupils. This is partly due to their memory and attention problems as well as being a byproduct of low self-esteem.
- Praise and rewards should be applied when a child has achieved a desired target. *Small and immediate rewards are more effective* than long-term or delayed rewards. It is important to remember that children with AD/HD are easily distracted, therefore, rewards should not be overly elaborate or likely to overshadow the task in any way. Rewards need to be as immediate as possible, since children with AD/HD often have problems with thinking outside of their immediate time frame.
- Negative consequences, in the form of mild punishment, can sometimes be effective. *They should be used sparingly, be clearly focused and highly specific.* For example, mild reprimands for being off task will be most effective when they involve a reminder of the task requirement. Thus it is better to say: 'please, stop talking and get back to reading page three of your history booklet', rather than, 'please get on with your work'. Their effectiveness will also be enhanced in classrooms where teachers are habitually positive in their behaviour towards children. It is interesting to note that students do not like to be told off by teachers who hold them in high regard; conversely, students often find it difficult to accept praise from teachers who habitually treat them with contempt or disrespect.
- Preferred activities (e.g. working on a computer) are more effective rewards than concrete rewards (e.g. sweets). Remember, however, it is *the child's preference* that counts here. For example, not all children see working on the computer as a treat: this may be especially true for a child who makes use of a computer as regular part of their learning programme

(as is the case for many children with literacy difficulties and AD/HD). For this reason, rewards should be negotiated with the pupil and rotated frequently to avoid loss of interest. *Develop a 'rewards menu'* which contains a variety of possible rewards.

- *Previewing and reviewing of tasks* helps pupils to know what is expected of them and to make sense of what they are doing.
- *'Priming'* helps motivate pupils with AD/HD. This involves previewing with the pupil the task and the likely rewards of successful completion.
- Interactions with pupils should be marked by *brevity, calmness and quietness*. Reprimands, where necessary, should be quiet and accompanied by direct eye contact.
- Children with attention problems are more forgetful than most children. Therefore, it is important to *avoid signs of exasperation* when repeating task requirements to pupils (e.g. 'if I've told you once I've told you a thousand times . . .'). Always give task requirements as though you are giving them for the first time, in a calm and measured way. Exasperation will be experienced as unfair by the child with AD/HD. Sarcasm is definitely not appropriate in these circumstances.
- Children with AD/HD perform best in *pair rather than group situations*. This is because there is a tendency for group situations to be overstimulating. In groups there tend to be too many possible distractions, and too much strain placed on the child's limited social skills.
- Difficulties with sequencing, concentration /distractibility make *writing a very difficult task* for children with AD/HD. Alternative means of presenting knowledge (e.g. through tape, use of amanuensis, and computer) can help here. Another important factor here is the need for the child to be *placed in a calm and quiet place*, where the often intense concentration required will not be threatened by noise or other distractions.
- *Simple behavioural interventions* (now well known to many UK teachers), if applied with great diligence, can be helpful in establishing and reinforcing behavioural requirements and boundaries, for example:

  - *Time out.* A place where the child can be sent for a short specified period (3 to 5 minutes) when he or she is misbehaving, where he or she will not receive stimulation or attention. Where this or any other punishment is used it should be clearly explained to the child (1) why it is being done, with direct reference to the offence, and (2) what it is intended to achieve (e.g. to give time for reflection, time to cool off). It is also important that when the time out period is over the teacher responds to the child with warmth and acceptance to indicate that the 'offence' has now been dealt with and can be put in the past in favour of current and more positive pursuits.
  - *Ignore-rules-praise.* In the behavioural sense, ignoring is the removal of attention that might act as reinforcement. It is not an act of rudeness whereby a child's attempts at positive interaction with the teacher are not responded to. Ignoring is always directed at the behaviour rather than the individual, and is most effectively employed in the guise of applying attention to a positive act that is taking place simultaneously with the negative act. The intended message here is: 'I am happy and eager to show attention and give praise to a child who is carrying out desirable behaviour. I find this much more valuable than negative behaviour'. If ignoring is carried out in a context where such positive attention is common it may lead to attention seeking behaviour.

Ignoring is only powerful in discouraging behaviour when it is understood by the child to be the absence of positive attention. This technique involves the teacher *ignoring* rule breaking behaviour, whilst *praising* another child who is obeying the rule, in a way that is clear to the misbehaving child. This should always involve a statement of the rule. Similarly, ignoring is only effective if the person whose behaviour is being ignored has experience of his or her positive behaviour being praised. Clearly this approach depends on the creation of a few simple, realistic, clearly stated rules.

– *Behavioural contracts*. This is another way of establishing expectations, discussing them with the child and reinforcing them. Here an agreement is made between the teacher and child (this can also involve parents) which establishes clear behavioural expectations, states how these are to be achieved and relates their achievement to particular reward. Rewards should be short term and low key (see above).

– *Token economies*. This involves the giving of tokens (in the form of points, stickers, or other 'currency') as rewards for positive rule compliant behaviour. These tokens are then exchanged for a more concrete reward (such as a preferred activity or more tangible reward).

● *Dialogue* between teacher and student should be an ongoing aspect of their daily interactions. This dialogue should be carried out in a way that expresses to the student the teacher's *empathy* and *positive regard* for the child. It is also important that the teacher be *honest* and avoid misleading the child about the desirability of anti-social or other negative behaviours. It comes naturally to some teachers to show a personal interest in their students, by asking them questions or sharing humour with them. *Non-sarcastic humour* is actually a low key way of expressing positive regard to another person. This dialogue helps the teacher to:

– monitor the child's mood state and feelings about the success or otherwise of the intervention programme;
– learn about personal, family and social factors that may influence the child's performance;
– detect learning difficulties;
– develop a positive relationship with the child, and
– model to the child and other children positive modes of interaction.

Dialogue between teacher and pupil, therefore, provides part of the basis for and one of the best means of meeting the child's needs. It also contributes to the child's sense of being valued, accepted and personal sense of security.

Thinking positively about AD/HD

So much of the phenomenon that we call AD/HD is associated with negativity and problems of some kind that it is very easy for people to become thoroughly fed up with the condition and the child who has it. There are no easy answers to this problem. Where this happens, however, the all-important relationship between the teacher and the student suffers. This in turn will often lead to an exacerbation of the child's unwanted behaviour and make the teacher even more fed up. In this section we look at ways in which some of the characteristics associated with AD/HD can be construed in more positive ways. The aim here is twofold:

1. To offer the teacher strategies for thinking positively when they can see only negativity.

2. To offer ways of thinking that can produce solutions to learning and behavioural problems.

The reframing technique

Children with AD/HD often come to be locked into cycles of negativity, whereby it seems that everything they do receives a negative response or reprimand. Teachers also can sometimes find themselves trapped into perpetuating these cycles. *Reframing* is a technique that has many valuable applications, especially when dealing with behavioural problems. It involves finding a *new* and *positive* way of thinking about a child's problem behaviour and has the effect of helping the teacher to break cycles of negativity.

Although this technique may at first appear to defy common sense, it should be pointed out that it is based on practices used by some clinical psychologists to great success with very severe emotional and behavioural disorders. These practices were adapted for educational settings by Molnar and Lindquist (1989).

It is vitally important to frame **all** pupils' behaviour as positively as possible. This is not the same as condoning unwanted or undesirable behaviour. It helps the teacher to suggest positive ways in which children might use certain of their characteristics. It also allows the teacher to indicate that although a behaviour may not be appropriate in one situation, there may be situations to which the behaviour is highly or at least more appropriate. This can have important consequences for:

- pupils' **self-esteem**;
- the development of **cooperative teacher–pupil relationships** in class, and
- changing behaviour.

Reframing undesirable behaviours in positive ways helps pupils to believe that:

- you like them
- you care about them

In using this technique it is important to avoid communicating *approval* of undersirable behaviour. It may well be the case that some forms of behaviour, such as those involving violence may not lend themselves to this technique. It is important to use the technique where it has a chance of being effective, and where it will be productive and convincing. Sometimes it may be appropriate to use the reframing technique in a way that also indicates a mild disapproval of the current behaviour. This can be done by providing a positive reframing of the unwanted behaviour and then indicating that there are situations, other than the present one, in which these qualities are more appropriately displayed.

For your reframing to be successful it must be:

- **convincing**, in that it fits the facts of the situation as student and teacher see them;
- done in a **genuine** way (without sarcasm), and

• be **congruent** with your way of behaving towards the student.

Table 4.1 shows some ways of framing AD/HD characteristics.

Table 4.1 Some negative and positive ways of framing characteristics of AD/HD (based on Hartmann, 1993)

Negative	Positive
Distractible	High level of environmental awareness
Short attention span, but with periods of intense focus	Responds well when highly motivated
Poor planner; disorganised; impulsive	Flexible; ready to change strategy quickly
Distorted sense of time	Tireless when motivated
Impatient	Goal oriented
Difficulty converting words into concepts	Visual/concrete thinker
Has difficulty following directions	Independent
Daydreamer	Bored by mundane tasks/ imaginative
Acts without considering consequences	Willing and able to take risks
Lacking in social skills	Single minded in pursuit of goals

These are some possible positive reframes for common classroom problems.

• Being out of seat too frequently:	energetic and lively
• Deviating from what the rest of the class is supposed to be doing:	independent, inquisitive, individualistic
• Talking out of turn or calling out:	keen to contribute
• Being aggressive toward classmate:	sensitive, emotional, passionate
• Losing and forgetting equipment:	thoughtful; absorbed in own ideas
• Handing in homework late or not at all:	perfectionist; unable to get started because of high standards
• Handing in incomplete or sloppy work:	signs of effort in spite of difficulties

Put simply children with AD/HD (like all children) perform most effectively when tasks are tailored to harness positive aspects of their characteristics and so prevent them from becoming dysfunctional. They are also likely to be more motivated when teachers and others behave towards them in ways that are positive and geared to enhancing their self esteem.

AD/HD and cognitive style

Cognitive style refers to the preferred ways individuals have of learning new information and skills. It is argued by some commentators on the subject that the symptoms of AD/HD are not those of a disorder at all, but that they are evidence of high creativity or simply a cognitive style that is different but of equal validity to the cognitive styles of other children (Crammond, 1994). This argument is probably an overstatement of the case. If a child's learning difficulties are simply a matter of cognitive style, then the child does not have AD/HD.
Different learning styles include:

1. A preference for learning for *concrete experience*
    Emphasises: feeling over thinking; here and now complexity over theories and generalisations; intuitive over systematic.

2. A preference for *reflective observation*
    Emphasises: understanding over practical application; the ideal over the pragmatic; reflection over action.

3. A preference for *abstract conceptualisations*
    Emphasises: thinking over feeling; theories over here and now complexity; systematic over intuitive.

4. A preference for *active experimentation*
    Emphasises pragmatic over ideal; doing rather than observing. (The typology of learning styles based on Kolb, 1984, pp.68-9)
    Children with AD/HD tend to favour the concrete experience learning style and the active. These learning styles are most useful in circumstances where tasks are experiential in nature: where the learning emerges from doing. There is still a tendency for schools, however, to focus on tasks which are essentially reflective and abstract, as is demonstrated by the general emphasis on the literary form in the National Curriculum and public examinations. Yet, it seems that much curriculum content can be approached by using any of these means.

> **Using Different Learning Styles to Teach the Same Content: an example**
>
> Aim: To enable pupils to understand the difference between short- and long-term consequences (in history).
>
> 1 Concrete experience:
> Teacher sets up role play involving a group of characters and a specific set of circumstances. The pupils are required to develop the scenario in terms of its consequences (a) after one hour; (b) consequences after10 years.
>
> 2 Reflective observation:
> Teacher asks pupils to read an account of the Black Death and its consequences, and to extract consequences and categorise them as short- and long-term.
>
> 3 Abstract conceptualisation:
> Teacher offers pupils an account of the Black Death and asks them to determine the *likely* short- and long-term consequences of the events decribed.
>
> 4 Active experimentation:
> Poses pupils the problem of: what events would be necessary in order to produce the short- and long-term outcomes associated with a particular, unidentified, historical event.

AD/HD and creativity

It is also true that many of the characteristics associated with AD/HD are also associated with high creativity. These are some of the ways in which traits associated with creativity and AD/HD overlap:

- self-centredness;
- emotionally hypersensitive;
- highly imaginative: 'in a world of their own';
- divergent thinking, and
- impulsive, spontaneous, unpredictable (Crammond, 1994; Jordan, 1992).

Of course being creative is no excuse for bad behaviour. If, however, a child's negative behaviour is associated with a high level of creativity it is likely that the child will benefit socially and educationally from opportunities to exercise their creativity positively. Creative students can often be a valuable resource to the classroom teacher in their ability to offer divergent ways of looking at things or novel approaches (and solutions) to problems. Openly acknowledging and giving status to a child's abilities in this area can again help to provide the child with a legitimate channel by which he or she can become positively involved in classroom activities.

Effective teaching in context: Whole school characteristics to help the child with AD/HD

Many of the above items are already in the repertoire of the effective classroom teacher, who combines knowledge of subject matter, teaching techniques, specific pupil characteristics and prevalent conditions to produce lessons that have clearly defined outcomes tailored to the differential needs of their pupils. What classroom teachers are able to achieve in the classroom is, of course, constrained by the broader school context. So here, finally, is a list of some of the whole school characteristics that will support these endeavours. Key issues here relate to the extent to which structures exist to identify and address problems as they arise.

- *Longer rather than shorter lesson blocks.* Efforts should be made to minimise the disruptive effects of too many lesson changes. At the same time the lessons themselves should be carefully structured to provide variety of activity and focus (as above).
- *Attention should be given to environmental distractors in school.* The primary function of the school is to enable teaching and to promote learning. If either of these functions is impaired by physical or environmental factors (such as preparations for lunch; maintenance to the building's fabric etc.) then it is necessary to reduce the effect of this impairment, or adjust expectations about teaching and learning quality.
- *Balancing physical and cognitive needs.* All children behave and attend better under conditions where their needs for physical activity are met. Concentration and application are aided by frequent opportunities for physical exercise. For example, one study found that a group of hyperactive children were able to sustain application and unbroken attention in class for periods of up to 40 minutes when given short breaks in which they could engage in physical activity.
- *Concentration of lessons requiring high levels of cognitive engagement earlier rather than later in the day.* Timetabling does not always make this possible, but it is important to bear in mind that people tend to be cognitively fresher earlier rather than later in the day. This is one of the benefits of the 'continental day' which may begin at 7.30 am but finish at 2 pm. Similarly, it is important to provide a balance in the educational diet so that whole days are not entirely devoted to cognitive activities or physical activities (Pelligrini and Horvat, 1995; Pelligrini *et al.*, 1996).
- *Teacher consultation on school management and curricular issues* is a common feature of well-run schools. Where channels of communication are open between senior managers and other staff. Without this kind of communication it is difficult for policies to be developed that reflect the everyday realities of classroom life. Of course, for this to be effective it requires that senior management be pro-active in carrying out consultation.
- *Pupil consultation on school management and curricular issues* echoes many of the points made under the previous heading. It should also be remembered that consultation is not the same as democracy. Consultation is about listening to others and explaining why decisions are made.
- *Positive parental involvement* requires that parents be made to feel welcome in the school, and that they are kept informed and consulted about school developments.
- *The sharing of pastoral and academic responsibilities throughout staff,* rather than having strict demarcation lines between pastoral and academic

responsibilties ensures that these two areas of interest do not conflict. So often do pastoral problems first manifest themselves as academic problems, whilst academic problems can lead to pastoral problems, that it is always necessary for staff to be prepared to deal with any situation.

- *All children benefit from effective whole school policies that:*

    - celebrate rather than stigmatise individual differences
    - allow pupils to gain recognition and high self-esteem from a wide range of activities (i.e. comprehensive reward structure)
    - provide effective learning and emotional/behavioural support where and when pupils need it

Summary

- Teachers should draw on behavioural methods to establish and reinforce clear rules and boundaries. They should be aware of modelling the kinds of behaviours they wish their students to perform.
- Main principles for behavioural intervention are to:

    - remove reason why a child might wish to avoid positive engagement in lessons
    - create circumstances in which positive attention is avaliable to children for legitimate reasons
    - ensure clear and effective channels of communication
    - cater for individual differences

- The child with AD/HD often has esteem problems. These can be addressed by teachers through the use of certain interpersonal techniques, such as:

    - empathy
    - unconditional positive regard
    - honesty
    - the reframing technique

- Children with AD/HD often favour particular learning styles, such as the concrete and active types. They may also have traits of high creativity. Knowledge of how to cater for these characteristics can be invaluable in meeting the child's educational needs.
- The social and educational needs of all children, especially those with AD/HD, are better catered for in classrooms and schools that have effective systems in place for:

    - minimising influences that interfere with learning processes
    - maximising the availability of conditions that take advantage of children's natural powers of attentiveness
    - maximising opportunities for staff and student involvement and sense of institutional ownership

References

Crammond, B (1994), The relationship between AD/HD and creativity, paper presented at the annual conference of the American Educational Research Association, New Orleans.

DuPaul, G and Stoner, G (1994), *AD/HD in the Schools: Assessment and Intervention Strategies*, New York, Guilford.

Hartmann, T (1993), *Attention Deficit Disorder: A Different Perception*, Novato, CA, Underwood-Miller.

Jordan, D (1992), *Attention Deficit Disorder: AD/HD and ADD Syndromes*, Austen, TX, Pro-Ed.

Kolb, D (1984), *Experience and Learning*, Englewood Cliffs,NJ, Prentice-Hall.

Molnar, A and Linquist, B (1989), *Changing Problem Behavior in Schools*, San Francisco, Jossey Bass.

Pellegrini, A and Horvat, M (1995), A developmental contextualist critique of Attention Deficit/Hyperactivity Disorder, *Educational Researcher*, **24**, No. 1, 13–20.

Pellegrini, A, Davis Huberty, P and Jones, I (1996), The effects of recess timing on children's playground and classroom behaviors,' *American Educational Research Journal*, **32**, No. 4, 845–64.

CHAPTER 5

Medication for AD/HD: Can it be justified?

Medication therapy is often used as a key component of AD/HD treatment, *although it should never be applied as the sole intervention*. Rather, it should be placed within a holistic treatment framework devised to address individual, functional difficulties, which will include psychological and social factors, as well as biological dimensions. This 'bio-psycho-social' approach consists of an integrated and coordinated programme of interventions to assist the child.

As most children with AD/HD spend their school careers in mainstream classrooms, all teachers are called upon to inform themselves about various AD/HD treatment strategies, including medication. Special needs teachers, who will likely be dealing with more extreme cases of AD/HD, will be involved with medication in the context of the more formalised structure of an individualised educational programme (IEP).

In this chapter, medication therapy is discussed in relation to its role in AD/HD treatment, including indications for considering use, various medications currently used in treatment, effects of various medications on AD/HD symptoms, long-term effects and side-effects, the importance of monitoring medication, the place of medication therapy in relation to other treatment modes, areas of controversy in relation to medication, and the proper role of the teacher in relation to this intervention.

The role of the teacher

Teachers can play several very significant roles in relation to medication therapy: (1) they can provide detailed information to the diagnosing physician and others on the assessment team (parents, educational psychologists, social workers) about the child's symptoms and difficulties prior to diagnosis, and (2) they can, indeed must, take an active role in the daily monitoring of medication effects observed in the classroom.

However, regarding the decision to medicate, it should always be understood that decisions to conduct a medication trial, adjust medication dosage or cease medication *are the purvue of the physician and parents*, hopefully incorporating teacher opinion. Professionalism requires that personal or philosophical objections to medication by teachers be set aside in favour of cooperating with the treatment plan, once agreed. A more detailed discussion of the teacher's role is provided at the end of this chapter, which enables the reader to incorporate information gained in the following sections into a clearer understanding of the teacher's responsibilities.

The role of medication in AD/HD treatment

Stimulant medication has been used to treat AD/HD symptoms since 1937. A physician (Bradley), working with children hospitalised for encephalitis who exhibited emotional and behavioural difficulties, employed the amphetamine, Benzedrine. Dramatic improvement in conduct and school performance was noticed. This led to further exploration of the effects of stimulant medications on individuals experiencing AD/HD-type symptoms due to disease or injury.

The stimulant, methylphenidate (trade name: Ritalin), now most commonly used to treat AD/HD, was released in 1957 for commercial use in the USA, although few scientific studies were then available. In the 1960s and 1970s this compound (which is *not* an amphetamine) came into increased use, leading to public controversy and intense political scrutiny, which in turn led to further scientific research into safety and effectiveness.

Widespread fears and controversies regarding the use of methylphenidate with children in the USA between the 1960s and the 1990s triggered extensive research, making it now 'the most well studied medication in childhood psychiatry' (Barkley, 1990). Thousands of scientific articles have published research findings related to medication treatment of AD/HD.

Psychostimulant medication is the most common AD/HD treatment in the USA, were approximately 2 per cent of school-aged children receive medication therapy annually (1988 figures). The average duration of medication treatment is between 2 and 7 years, depending on age at diagnosis. Ninety per cent of children diagnosed with AD/HD receive medication therapy in the USA, and of that number, the vast majority are prescribed stimulants to increase arousal levels in the central nervous system (CNS).

Growing acceptance of AD/HD as a chronic, developmental condition, affecting individuals over the lifespan, is increasing overall prescription rates in the general population as adults are now being diagnosed later in life. It is the case that many parents of children with AD/HD have struggled with emotional and behavioural difficulties themselves, and through knowledge gained in their child's assessment, eventually discover their own disability.

Understanding the role of medication in AD/HD treatment requires understanding that the condition is multidimensional and developmental, comprised of biological, psychological, social and cultural elements. For illustration, consider the following as typical in individuals whose AD/HD is not identified, or goes untreated.

Over time, a neurologically distressed, biologically vulnerable infant evolves into a 'difficult' child, whose fragile self esteem and tenuous coping skills are continuously damaged by high levels of adult censure/criticism and peer rejection. This 'difficult' child slowly metamorphasises into a disaffected teen, burdened by entrenched 'bio-psycho-social' patterns of childhood difficulty, which in turn become further reinforced in the course of normal adolescent developmental stresses. This 'EBD youth' may later emerge from the developmental chrysalis as a troubled adult with numerous, interwoven life difficulties, including: a chronic, diminished sense of self-worth reinforced through years of negative social feedback; a negative, defeatist view of life that undermines motivation and achievement; a lack of hope for, or confidence in future improvement; and underdeveloped coping abilities in cognitive, emotional and behavioural terms. In terms of overall personality development then, the adult with AD/HD is likely to have serious, ongoing problems in every aspect of life functioning, including: self-management, relationships and marriage, parenting, and employment. Some would argue that this is a recipe for additional 'co-morbid' problems, e.g. depression, suicide, family violence, divorce, unemployment or underemployment, delinquency, criminality and a plethora of other personal and social ills.

This rather grim scenario is, of course, painted in extreme terms, and is by no means inevitable. What it does provide, however, to teachers, parents, and others interested in children with AD/HD or other forms of EBD, is a set of sobering and compelling reasons for devising and implementing strategies to help - and to help as early as possible in the individual's life. In the case of AD/HD, it seems that 'an ounce of prevention is [surely] worth a pound of cure.'

The picture *is not hopeless*, nor should it be taken as a doomsday scenario. However, it points to the need, as noted in the discussion regarding the importance of personal beliefs, values, and attitudes, for adults working with such children to identify and clarify their views about the use of medication. It is critical for teachers and others to take a long view in terms of weighing their perspectives about this subject. In the short term, or in immediate term, most adults would prefer to avoid prescribing medication to manage a child's behaviour. That is why it is so important, when attempting to understand the role of medication in the much larger context of multi-modal AD/HD intervention, to balance the distaste for medical interventions against the developmental backdrop of the individual's life. When the potential risks associated with untreated AD/HD are held against the natural concerns for the child's safety and well being, many parents and teachers accept that, in a less than perfect world, it is preferable to medicate as part of a coordinated programme of psychological, social and educational strategies aimed at the whole child. *The whole child must be helped*, and in many cases, medication, appropriately prescribed and monitored, will be part of a strategic plan to provide critical environmental interventions. The child's eventual experiences will most likely be best helped by developing psychological and social coping skills that medication can pave the way for in the classroom.

When is medication necessary?

The decision to prescribe stimulant medication should be directly linked to thorough, precise and accurate assessment-diagnosis procedures. *A decision to initiate medication therapy should never be taken as an automatic response to a diagnosis of AD/HD.*

Factors to consider before attempting medication therapy are suggested by Barkley (1990):

1. Severity of the AD/HD symptoms and behaviour.

2. Prior experience with other treatments.

3. Presence of anxiety disorder symptoms.

4. Parental attitudes towards medication.

5. Availability and adequacy of adult supervision.

6. Child's attitudes towards medication.

Types of medication used to treat AD/HD

The vast majority of AD/HD sufferers are treated with CNS stimulants, regardless of the presence or absence of hyperactivity. Historically, research into medication use for AD/HD has been primarily conducted in reference to hyperactivity, and associated externalising problems. Stimulants have been shown to produce favourable, short-term results in 70-80 per cent of children studied. However, non-hyperactive children, who are more likely to have internalising problems, have been shown to respond less well to stimulants. Studies continue of this latter group into the effectiveness of various antidepressants, sometimes used successfully in combination with stimulants. In sum, research establishing the short-term effectivenes of stimulants in helping children diminish AD/HD symptoms is robust. However, insufficient research as to long-term benefits has been conducted. In the remainder of this chapter specific medications used to treat AD/HD are described.

Central Nervous System (CNS) stimulants

Methylphenidate is by far the most widely prescribed medication for AD/HD treatment, with 90 per cent of children prescribed stimulants receiving it, as opposed to other types. It is sold under the trade name 'Ritalin.' Two forms of Ritalin are available in the USA: short acting (tablets of 5, 10 and 20 mg having a behavioural effect duration of 3–4 hours) and long acting (Ritalin-SR) (tablets of 20 mg having a behavioural effect duration of 7 hours). A few studies report that the long acting version may not be as effective. This is balanced by the fact that a single dosage given in the morning eliminates the need for the child to go to the school nurse at midday to obtain the second dose, an activity which often results in the child being singled out and stigmatised by peers. At the time of writing, only the short acting tablets are available in the UK.

Ritalin is a highly regulated drug worldwide because, like many medications, can be misused and abused. As an effective CNS stimulant it has a black market appeal and a history of illicit use. It is important to note that misuse and abuse of methylphenidate/Ritalin is almost exclusively reported among individuals *not* under treatment for AD/HD. Studies of children and adolescents treated appropriately with methylphenidate have shown they are no more prone to dependency or addiction than others, perhaps less so because (1) they do not experience the effects as a 'drug high', (2) they do not view it as a way to rebel or gain early adult status because they have taken it often for many years, and (3) they often experiment with *not* taking it in the teen years because it either makes them feel different from their peers, or because they are seeking to show adults they can perform without it as a form of self-assertion. Not taking their prescribed Ritalin can become a form of adolescent rebellion against adult demands, in a similar way that using or abusing drugs can be for teens without AD/HD.

Almost all medications can have side effects for someone. Common side effects of Ritalin *may* include insomnia, appetite depression, weight loss, headache, irritability and stomach ache, usually experienced as the medication dose is wearing off. It is not recommended in patients with marked anxiety, motor tics or with a family history of Tourette syndrome.

Dextro-amphetamine ('Dexedrine') is a central nervous system (CNS) stimulant. Like methylphenidate, it is legally restricted, thus not available over-the-counter, but rather falls under prescribing guidelines like Ritalin. However, in the USA, d-amphetamine is the only stimulant approved for children aged 3–6 years old (although warnings are issued with this and other similar stimulant medications advising against this practice). It is manufactured in various forms, including 5 mg tablets, 5, 10, 20 spansules, and elixir. Tablets are short acting (3–4 hours behavioural effect duration), whilst spansules are long acting (10–13 hours). This medication has similar side effects and precautions as those of methylphenidate.

Pemoline, ('Cylert'), is another stimulant medication, but one which is less frequently used than Dexedrine. It is less preferred and is usually prescribed only when trials of the other stimulants show them to be ineffective. There are two reasons for this: one is that pemoline can take from 2–4 weeks to show a clinical response, whereas the other medications act immediately, and the second is that this medication may in rare cases be associated with liver failure. Warnings issued with this medication advise regular blood monitoring of liver function, or avoidance in individuals with a history of liver disease/dysfunction.

Pemoline tablets are long acting, and of three dosage strengths: 18.75 mg, 37.5 mg and 75 mg, which are in effect in a range of 12–24 hours. It is given once per day, beginning with a trial dosage of 56–150 mg in children. Pemoline-treated children have been shown to experience short term growth suppression which evens out in the long term.

Caffeine is a widely used CNS stimulant which is not a prescription medication. It was researched as a possible AD/HD treatment in the 1970s because of its common sense appeal. It was reasoned by some that its stimulant properties should be effective in reducing or eliminating AD/HD symptoms. Studies comparing the effects of caffeine on AD/HD symptoms with those of prescription stimulants found either no effects or slight improvements not evaluated as significantly effective. Thus, by the 1980s, caffeine was not seriously considered to be a useful treatment.

Antidepressants

A second class of medication - tricyclic antidepressants - is more recently being used to treat ADHD. This category includes *imiprimine* (Tofranil) and *desipramine* (Norpramin), which produce behavioural effects similar to the CNS stimulants in children with AD/HD. Both medications have been found to decrease parent and teacher ratings of inattention, hyperactivity and aggression in up to 70 per cent of patients, however neither has been shown to enhance cognitive functioning as do stimulants. The tricyclic antidepressants are slower acting, and are usually prescribed to children who either do not respond to stimulants, or who have pre-existing or coexisting symptoms of anxiety or clinical depression. Both types are available in tablets ranging in dosage from 10 mg to 150 mg, and can produce similar side effects, including dry mouth, decreased appetite, headache, stomachache, dizziness, constipation or mild tachycardia.

Other prescription medications

Clonidine hydrochloride ('Catapress'), an antihypertensive (blood pressure) drug, has been recently added to the pharmacopaeia of AD/HD medications. Its action is believed to be similar to that of the stimulants, and it has an advantage of skin patch administration. Although it is used to treat Tourette's syndrome (TS) and thus appears to be useful in treating AD/HD where tics or TS are present (prohibiting stimulant therapy), its value as a medical treatment of AD/HD is yet to be determined with confidence or certainty as it is not well studied at present.

How stimulant medications work

Current use of stimulants to treat AD/HD is based on recently refined, yet not totally conclusive, theories of its causation. These theories suggest that the range of emotional and behavioural difficulties incorporated in the AD/HD diagnosis are rooted in biochemical disturbances in the normal functions of the brain's frontal lobe. While such disturbances can result from brain injury, disease, lead ingestion, and alcohol/drug abuse, experts believe that, in the vast majority of cases, AD/HD is genetically inherited.

Certain brain chemicals (neurotransmitters) are responsible for relaying information between/among various parts of the brain. They are necessary for certain functions to take place properly, such as impulse control, concentration, and motor regulation. Dysregulation in this complex chemical relay system can and does appear as emotional and behavioural aberration. Stimulant medications, such as Ritalin, are employed not to sedate overactive or inattentive children, but as a chemical facilitator that raises chronically low levels of activity in certain parts of the brain, and so regulates the message carrying process in individuals whose natural abilities are impaired.

Effects of medication on AD/HD symptoms

The symptoms of AD/HD are thought to arise from a state of chronic 'underarousal' of portions of the brain regulating emotional and behavioural response. The problems and difficulties of individuals with AD/HD are typically seen in the areas of self control impaired by the chemically caused underarousal. Psychostimulant medications are so named because of their ability to stimulate parts of the brain

Dramatic and immediate effects of stimulant medication on AD/HD symptoms are well established in scientific literature. This is a result of numerous rigorous studies conducted worldwide. Barkley (1990) observes that, even by the end of the 1970s, 'this treatment approach [was] the most well-studied therapy in child psychiatry'.

Effects of the medication on AD/HD symptoms are usually discussed as consisting of two main types: *short-term* and *long-term effects*. These categories refer to immediate and eventual effects that are desired, whereas *side effects*, which can occur with any medication therapy, are those effects seen as undesirable, perhaps harmful in the short or long term. There are also effects which are considered to be *primary*, or direct, and *secondary*, or indirect *effects*. Each of these categories is discussed in the following sections.

Side effects

As in the case of any medication or medical treatment, side effects (neutral or undesirable results associated with the medication) can also occur. The possible disadvantages of prescribing stimulant medications must always be weighed and balanced against anticipated positive results. This task is within the role of the prescribing physician in ongoing consultation with parents and children, with appropriate advice from teachers who have first-hand knowledge of the child's response, gained from conscientious classroom observation over time.

Despite valid short term gains consistently reported in 70–80 per cent of cases in which stimulants are administered, disadvantages and difficulties can and do occur. Unwanted side effects often signal the need to adjust dosage and in some cases may indicate the need to stop administration of a particular medication, or to change to a different one.

Parents, children and teachers must be aware of possible negative side effects and monitor progress in this area consistently and cooperatively, so that reliable feedback about medication effects can be regularly provided to the prescribing physcian. Details on the full nature of the teacher's role in relation to medication therapy are discussed later in this chapter.

One disadvantage of medication therapy is its lack of effectiveness in a small but significant percentage of inattentive children. The 20–30 per cent for whom desired effects (not necessarily negative or harmful side effects, but no appreciable effects) do not result are obviously not helped in ways that medication 'responders' are. These 'non-responders' challenge parents, teachers and clinicians to devise behavioural, environmental and cognitive intervention plans that exclude medication as a component.

Unwanted side effects of stimulant medications can include potentially irreversible problems with tics (usually in individuals with pre-existing, complicating medical conditions, such as seizure disorders or Tourette's Syndrome). This risk factor mandates close, continuous monitoring throughout the administration period by individuals in direct daily contact with the child.

Fears about diminished growth patterns in children treated with stimulant medications surfaced in the 1970s, and this topic has been widely studied as a result. Because in some children anorexia or appetite depression occur, even in combination with desired effects related to diminishing AD/HD symptoms, concerns about long-term growth suppression are often expressed in relation to medication treatment. Height and weight are the two factors used to evaluate the effects of stimulant medications on normal growth patterns in treated children.

Two decades of well-designed studies indicate that growth retardation is *not* a significant risk factor, although in some cases children under 10 years of age show a transient decrease in weight and slight growth slowing, which later normalise. A common practice has been to initiate medication 'holidays' during summer holiday periods, as a few studies showed that growth patterns evened out during this time. But more recently, experts increasingly agree that positive (secondary) effects (improved peer and family relationships) of remaining on medication outweigh concerns about possible growth suppression.

In a few people, methylphenidate may aggravate symptoms of anxiety, tension and agitation as well as having adverse effects on patients known to be clinically depressed, suffering from glaucoma, or with other psychiatric diagnoses, such as paranoia or schizophrenia. As with many other medications, stimulant medication therapy is not advised during pregnancy or in patients with histories of convulsive disorders. Ritalin can also interact with other medications in ways that can be aversive to patients, and should not be administered or taken without complete review of other agents being prescribed or consumed.

In addition to consultation with the physician and chemist, two direct sources of advice on stimulant medications, including Ritalin, are available to parents and teachers. The first is *The Physician's Desk Reference* (1989), a guide for prescribing medications widely used by American doctors, which describes in detail the medicine's properties, research findings about its actions and possible side effects, as well as 'contra-indications,' - those situations or patient characteristics which suggest it should not be used. Also, drug manufacturers provide patient advice of much the same type specific to each medicine.

For example, the written parent advice provided with each Ritalin prescription gives information on its chemical composition and intended use, warnings about pre-existing conditions of which the doctor should be aware before prescribing, warnings about other medicines being taken that could affect the results, directions for taking the tablets, and possible side effects to watch for. This same advice should always be made available to classroom teachers, whose daily observation of the child, in combination with that of parents, forms the basis of continuous medication monitoring. It is therefore critical that teachers educate themselves about medications in use for AD/HD in the normal course of maintaining and updating their professional currency.

The importance of monitoring medication

All medicines have the potential to produce unexpected or unwanted results in some cases, and AD/HD medication therapy is not an exception. Also, some medications are not effective in certain individuals, whereas, in other circumstances, complicating factors make AD/HD medication therapy more difficult.

Ongoing medication monitoring is vital and integral to effective AD/HD treatment. All adults interacting with a child undergoing medication therapy have a direct and ongoing responsibility to fulfil their role to observe and report on behavioural effects noted in relation to medication dosage.

No medication 'cures' AD/HD. The aim of medication therapy, regardless of the type used, is to eliminate or reduce primary neurological symptoms, in order to obtain secondary results: clear access to the learning/social situation and emotional/behavioural self control that leads to improved cognitive performance as well as improved family relations and greater peer acceptance. No medication in current use produces permanent changes in the brain neurochemistry believed to underly AD/HD. The condition is thus one that is managed in most children by a team of adults cooperating to insure greater chances for success in academic, social and interpersonal terms. In the cases in which AD/HD persists into adulthood to a level of chronic disorder impairing relationships, social and occupational performance, the individual must assume responsibility for medication therapy supervised by a physician. Children with AD/HD who have grown into adults still requiring medication therapy will hopefully enter their adult years with cognitive, behavioural and emotional strategies which have been learned and practiced with the support of medication therapy.

For this to effectively happen, teachers and parents must act in authentic partnership to monitor medication continuously. This effectively requires daily observation and analysis of the child's mood and behaviour states during those periods in which the dosage is in effect. Every effort to report objective , rather than subjectively should be made.

Medication in relation to other treatment modes

Medication paves the way for other treatment strategies to be applied and monitored. It should never be applied as a sole intervention, but always in combination with an individualised programme of strategies known as a 'multimodal' approach. This approach consists of interventions applied at various levels of functioning, including biological, psychological, social and cultural.

As previously noted, children with AD/HD have many emotional, behavioural and cognitive difficulties set in motion by the interaction of their neurologicial characteristics with environmental demands/conditions. Individual impairment may occur at mild, moderate or serious levels, and may or may not include hyperactivity as a feature. Other biological, psychological and social processes affect the ongoing course of the disorder, and may include specific learning difficulties, anxiety, depression, psychosis, or family and community disruption. Over time core AD/HD difficulties interact and compound if untreated, so that by adolescence and adulthood, severe problems are interwoven in seemingly inpenetrable layers. Medication in combination with other approaches can help the individual to be 'present' cognitively in such a way that learning of adaptive strategies can occur.

Myths and controversies in relation to medication and AD/HD

The use of medication in treating AD/HD has been widely debated in the past, and is still controversial for a variety of real and imagined reasons. Some myths and controversies persist and are periodically revived, usually in the popular press. Because, like any medical treatment, medication can cause unwanted side effects or prove altogether ineffective in a few cases, it is those cases that are most often used in the attempt to 'prove' the myth, and thus discredit this form of treatment. They are referred to as myths because scientific research conducted to evaluate their authenticity has consistently shown them to be unsubstantiated. This does not, however, appear to diminish their popularity in some quarters.

Three of the most common 'medication myths' are:

1. *Ritalin turns children into 'zombies.'*

   Hundreds, if not thousands of scientific studies have been conducted on the safety and effectiveness of methylphenidate, to the satisfaction of governmental regulating bodies in many countries. However, just because a medication is demonstrated as 'safe and effective' is no guarantee that (a) someone, somewhere, may not have an individual adverse reaction, (b) that all physicians never make errors in prescribing, (c) that everyone will respond equally to recommended dosages, or (d) that everyone takes medication exactly as prescribed. Human error, failure to monitor responses adequately, and individual biological differences can result in children appearing to be sedated or overly passive to observers. The literature suggests that this is almost always the result of problems of dosage adjustment and monitoring.

2. *Medication is a 'cure' for AD/HD.*

   Because AD/HD is considered to be a medical condition, albeit with important psycho-social dimensions, it is tempting to assume that a medication might quickly and easily reduce or eliminate the symptoms. This is certainly the case in some medical conditions. However, as in many other medical conditions, medications are used to 'manage' — but do not have the power to prevent or permanently 'cure'.

   For example, most people at some time suffer from a headache. They are able to 'manage' the headache by means of medication, in that in some cases it goes away permanently, sometimes it subsides until the dosage wears off, and sometimes it persists, despite all efforts. Although people know that some medications can alleviate individual headaches, they do not expect that one medication dosage, or even several, will prevent future headaches. Thus it is with AD/HD. Medication can reduce symptoms as long as it is properly administered and active within the individual's system. It cannot, however, remove the AD/HD or prevent its symptoms from arising again as soon as the dosage is worn off.

3. *Medication therapy will lead to drug dependence or addiction later in life.*

   Any medication can be misused or abused, as previously noted. It is difficult not to worry that treating children and adolescents with a powerful stimulant medication will not lead directly to physical and psychological dependency, or later drug addiction. Research into these questions has consistently led experts to conclude that it is individuals who are *not* treated for their AD/HD who are at the greater risk for drug dependency and addiction problems later in life. Those who are treated with medication appear more likely to accept it as a necessary medicine rather than seek thrills from it as an illicit drug. Further, they often seek to reduce or eliminate medication because their experience does not have pleasant connotations to them, and they seek 'normality' through not using it.

It is very important, however, to note, that psychological dependency can occur in some individuals, if other treatment strategies are not offered, or if proper education about the medication is not provided. If individuals are not advised that their improved behaviour and achievements are their own, but come to believe them to be the result of the medication rather than of their own effort whilst having the assistance of the medication's effects, problems can arise. It is the job of parents, teachers and doctors to teach personal responsibility and to reward positive results in such a way that the individual understands that the medication is not responsible, but that he or she is.

The teacher's role related to AD/HD medication therapy

Teachers and parents share a critical role in relation to medication therapy. As partners with a shared interest in helping the child achieve positive academic, social and personal results, they must work together cooperatively. It is important that this relationship is positive and that they do not fall into the common trap of viewing each other as adversaries. Teachers must come to view parents' concerns, interests, observations and intentions positively, and vice versa.

Next to parents, it is the teacher who interacts most directly with the medicated child on a day-to-day basis. In fact, because often parents may only see the child before the medication takes effect daily (morning, before school) and after its effects are worn off (after school, evenings), teachers are sometimes the primary observer and reporter of medication effects.

Thus, teachers are ideally and logistically positioned in respect to several aspects of medication therapy. The role of the teacher may be broken down into three main activities: (a) objective observer, (b) information collator and (c) team reporter. These activities require the teacher to be:

1. educated about the specific properties, actions and effects of various commonly prescribed medications used to treat AD/HD;

2. knowledgeable of the symptoms, characteristics and traits of AD/HD, and ways in which commonly used medications are used to eliminate, diminish or manage them;

3. clear about the specific, anticipated medication results aimed for with the individual child, and

4. willing to communicate regularly with parents and physicians as members of the team with commonly agreed goals.

In the observer mode, the teacher actively observes the child's progress in relation to behavioural, cognitive and emotional aims. These observations should be as objectively arrived at as possible, and reflect actual behaviours of the child rather than emotional impressions of the teacher. Although this can be difficult at first, precision is gained with practice and experience.

In the beginning stages of AD/HD therapy, medication monitoring should take place only after the teacher has had an opportunity to observe the child in a nonmedicated state. This early observation enables the teacher to establish a benchmark, against which subsequent observations and interpretations are made with regard to the medication's effectiveness and usefulness. It is also important to be aware that medication expectations for hyperactive and nonhyperactive types may vary considerably.

In the information collator role, the teacher will continuously organise and analyse information gathered through direct observation. This will be useful in the day-to-day classroom management of the case, as well as to assist other team members in keeping abreast of developments over time.

In the team reporter role, the teacher acts as the day-to-day observer of the child's behaviours in a similar way to parents. The information observed and collated is kept on file and made available in verbal or written report format to colleagues on the provision team.

Summary

- Medication has a relatively long history as a reliable treatment for the symptoms of AD/HD.
- The most common form of medication used with children is methylphenidate ('Ritalin'). This is a psychostimulant that has been repeatedly shown to have the effect of correcting the neurological understimulation that is believed to cause the primary symptoms of AD/HD.
- In a minority of cases other forms of medication are used, such as anti-depressants.
- There can be undesirable side effects from the use of methylphenadate. Mild but not harmful side effects, such as reduced appetite and mild sleep disturbance are relatively common. The more serious side effects can be avoided as a result of an effective assessment process which will indicate aspects of medical history that are associated with the worst side effects, and thus make medication an unwise option. The milder, more common side effects can be controlled by adjusting the dosage.
- Medication is almost never a sufficient treatment in itself for AD/HD. It must always be prescribed in conjunction with other forms of intervention, such as psychological, social and educational, which help the sufferer to develop skills, attitudes and behaviours that will enable them to cope with the demands of everyday life.

Questions

1. What sort of concerns do you have about the use of the kind of medication described for AD/HD, and with children?

2. In what circumstances do you think it is appropriate to use *any* form of medication in everyday life? What other forms of medication might methylphenidate be compared with?

3. On the basis of what you have read is the use of medication justified for children with AD/HD?

4. If a teacher disagreed with the use of medication, whilst the parent and the doctor were in favour of it:

   – what would be an appropriate action by the teacher?
   – what should the school's policy be in these circumstances?

CHAPTER 6

But what about . . .? AD/HD and other issues

There are many different aspects to AD/HD. It is impossible in a short book such as this to deal in detail with the rich diversity of perspectives on and ideas about this topic. In this chapter we deal with some of the many issues that are not dealt with in detail elsewhere in the book, but which may in one way or another influence the teacher's ability to deal effectively with the problems that AD/HD brings into the classroom.

Some popular misconceptions and controversies

AD/HD is not a straightforward topic. There are many different aspects to it, and many different ways of approaching it. An interesting and sometimes alarming aspect of the AD/HD idea is the way in which it seems to generate strong feelings of on the one hand, antipathy, and the other, almost religious fervour. Those who strongly oppose the concept of AD/HD sometimes do so on the basis of one or more of the following grounds:

- it is an American fad or scientifically dubious concept;
- an attempt to hide the true causes of psycho-social disorder, which are environmental and social, and place the responsibility for these problems on individual pathology;
- an excuse for poor parenting and ineffective schools;
- a convenient excuse used by parents to gain access to scarce resources, and protect their ill-motivated, anti-social children from the consequences of their actions;
- an excuse to control and suppress the natural exuberance and spontaneity of creative and independent children through the use of powerful drugs, and
- a means of controlling potentially troublesome nonconforming people.

On the other hand there are those who embrace the concept of AD/HD uncritically, sometimes seeing it as:

- underlying nearly all failures of personal motivation and disorganised behaviour;
- an explanation for all aspects of an individual's social, educational and professional failure;
- the single factor at the basis of school failure and criminal behaviour;
- an indicator of superior attributes which make the bearer the member of an exclusive club, and

- conclusive proof of the inaccuracy of environmental explanations for school failure and behavioural problems, and the validity of biological and genetic explanations for these outcomes.

The problem with all of these propositions is that they are often inaccurate and, more importantly, unhelpful, especially to the people who experience problems related to AD/HD. Like anything else, AD/HD is open to abuse. Unlike some other things when used properly AD/HD is very useful.

Important points to make in response to the misconceptions set out above are:

- The AD/HD concept has a long and respectable scientific pedigree, supported by international research studies, mainly in the areas of neuroscience and psychiatry.
- The value of the diagnosis lies not in fact that it diminishes the importance of environmental influences, rather the value of the AD/HD diagnosis lies in the light that it sheds on the ways in which the environment can affect the individual with the condition.
- Far from providing an excuse for not doing anything, the AD/HD diagnosis provides parents, teachers and other professionals with clear indications of how they should act to help the child develop in positive ways.
- An essential condition for the diagnosis to be applied is evidence that the child is failing socially and educationally as a result of the condition. Therefore, the aims of intervention should always be to help the child enjoy a happier, more successful life, in terms of social relationships and academic achievement.
- The aims of intervention should never be to suppress or otherwise impair a child's spontaneity, creativity or independence, but should always be to help the child to find ways of employing these qualities in ways that contribute to his or her social and academic success.
- The genetic aspect of AD/HD should not be assumed to point to the fact that all crime and deviance are the simple product of 'bad genes'. The genetic argument should be taken to indicate that just as poverty and deprivation place their victims at increased risk of psychological and social difficulty (including crime), there are certain aspects of human biology that may place certain individuals at greater risk than others for the same problems. The civilised message to be drawn from this is that just as we attempt to avert the socially disastrous effects of poverty and deprivation through social interventions that make success and happiness in life more accessible to the poor and deprived (e.g. through the provision of 'free' education and health services), so an understanding of conditions like AD/HD help us to create social circumstances and other opportunities for people with the condition that enable them to be happy and successful in the school, the peer group and family.
- AD/HD should never be a subject for maudlin pity, celebration or social avoidance. It should be recognised for what it is: a potentially serious and highly debilitating condition that if ignored or misunderstood can create misery and failure in the lives of people affected by it.
- Similarly, AD/HD should never be confused with temporary or trivial habits of disorganisation, inattentiveness or over activity. When AD/HD

requires professional intervention it is not a set of endearing traits of the type associated with the stereotypical 'absent minded professor' or 'life and soul of the party'. People with genuine, untreated primary AD/HD rarely become professors, and seldom get invitations to parties.

Gender and AD/HD

Until very recently, AD/HD was mainly conceptualised as hyperactivity in male children. It was also thought to be a short-term, developmental problem of childhood which somehow resolved itself during puberty, through unknown means. Indeed, it has historically been overactive boys, showing persistent anti-social or aggressive behaviours and academic difficulties, who have been studied most, and who are most likely to have received the diagnosis. Because such boys often made trouble for themselves and others, they typically form the basis of popular beliefs and stereotypes about the condition.

Emerging scientific research evidence, now compiled over many decades, is revealing a more sobering picture. Hyperactivity in male children is now viewed as only one aspect of a broader and more pervasive problem. Recognition of a broad spectrum of emotional and behavioural difficulties has replaced conceptualisations of it as a motor control problem, to include inattention and impulse control deficits. In addition, not all boys grow out of these problems, as, despite the recession of motor hyperactivity with age, they often become adolescents and men with chronic, debilitating emotional, social and occupational problems. Their primary, neurological differences , unless helped, predictably give rise to secondary emotional, academic and social problems. Further, with the shift in defining the central underlying feature away from hyperactivity to impulsivity and inattention, research is showing now that females are likely to suffer from AD/HD to a similar extent as males.

Studies of sex differences among children and adolescents diagnosed with AD/HD indicate that, in the absence of hyperactivity, the ratio of boys to girls affected by impulsivity and inattention is about 1:1. Thus, girls and women are just as likely to have ADD/without hyperactivity, as are boys and men. In addition, females can indeed also be physically hyperactive, although this type is much less often encountered.

Jordan (1992) describes non-hyperactive children as 'lost youngsters who drift and float quietly on the edges of the environment.' This image is reinforced by traditional social assumptions, values and ideals about how girls and women should be and behave. Passivity, docility, day-dreaminess, and 'muddle-headedness' are traits that society historically assigned the 'fairer sex' — and rewarded. Until recently, social assertiveness, academic achievement, occupational striving, and emotional reticence have not been considered desirable female traits. This, combined with rigid prescriptions/expectations that women opt out of the public sphere of life in favour of childbearing and childrearing, has created a social milieu in which social expectations and female role definitions were not challenged significantly by AD/HD characteristics.

In today's society, in which social, academic and occupational success are defined in more traditionally male terms, and applied to, and accepted by women as well as men, AD/HD in females may create different life difficulties. Women must now acquire the same levels of educational and occupational success as males in the current culture. Dependency in females is not valued as it once was. Despite recent media attention about the overall increasing school results of girls compared with boys, the modern classroom places the same demands on girls with AD/HD as on boys with the disorder. Thus, girls with AD/HD face similar difficulties, yet often without gaining the attention of parents and teachers.

A hallmark of AD/HD without hyperactivity is disorganisation, rather than overactivity. Difficulty with synthesising information and organising ideas, coupled with confusion — a kind of 'fogginess' — makes these pupils seem even more puzzling than hyperactive ones. Often the child is of average ability, or above average ability, but seems always to lag behind, unable to respond to seemingly simple requests or directions. The problem in this case is that society, including teachers, associate intelligence with quick mental processing speed.

A common problem for those without hyperactivity is that they are bright but slow. This anomaly is not usually understood, or accepted, thus such a child is quickly labelled uncooperative, attention seeking, lazy, obstinate, dull or disinterested. In cases in which specific learning difficulties, such as dyslexia, or other language processing problems, are present, this pupil is at an additional disadvantage. This pupil may slowly ebb away academically and socially, attracting little attention and no help, because he or she is not making trouble in the classroom.

So, what might a girl with AD/HD look like in the classroom? She will be chronically disorganised, a poor speller, shy, confused, and often ignored by peers. However, because some girls also have 'hyperactive' brains rather than overactive bodies, some may also be overly talkative, in ways that actually disturb others. In addition to her primary problems rooted in neurological dysfunction, over time it is likely she will develop secondary emotional and social problems as well. The nature of these secondary problems appears to differ from those acquired by males, in that aggression is more likely to be absent. Most girls with AD/HD struggle silently, ignored by teachers and peers, falling behind socially and academically. In adolescence, they have poor self-esteem, accrued over the years, and may turn to substance abuse and sexual promiscuity in an effort to gain peer acceptance.

AD/HD and adults

AD/HD traits have always been with us — they are not new. What is new is the attempt to describe, analyse and modify them in scientific terms, rather than in mystical or moralistic terms. As described in Chapter 1, science has attempted to understand the root of this disorder for well over a century, with growing levels of theoretical clarity and diagnostic precision.

Science now points to a relationship between AD/HD and many adult dysfunctions in individuals diagnosed earlier in life. It is only very recently that the study of AD/HD has suggested that in a significant proportion of cases these immature traits actually reflect the persistence of AD/HD into chronological adulthood.

Children with AD/HD are identified and eventually diagnosed on the basis that certain emotional and behavioural traits are immature when compared with age-matched peers. Sometimes AD/HD is described as a problem of developmental delay, in that their abilities to sustain attention, control impulses and manage motor activity are significantly under-developed when held against 'normal' age-mates.

When hyperactivity was considered by experts to be the central, defining problem, it was also believed that the disorder only affected children. Research is clear that motor hyperactivity diminishes considerably with age in all children, so that by adolescence and adulthood, it has diminished or subsided. Using this line of reasoning, in the 1960s and 1970s, scientists hypothesised that hyperactivity was an age-limited disorder. They further asserted that unclear biochemical processes triggered at puberty must be responsible for the 'spontaneous remission' of hyperactivity.

Studies of brain development and function, combined with genetic research, in the 1980s, expanded the conceptualisation of the problem as hyperactivity to the problem as AD/HD, encompassing a broader spectrum of difficulties. Since then, theorists have shifted their emphasis to asserting impulsivity as the main feature. This revised diagnostic framework furthered understanding of the way in which the syndrome can affect individuals well into adolescence and adulthood. In fact, this shift is the basis for emerging claims that AD/HD can be a 'lifelong' problem for many individuals.

Earlier theories that AD/HD only exists in children have now been refuted by studies showing that between 30–70 per cent of diagnosed children have either the full syndrome or significant residual symptoms into adulthood. These residual problems, whilst varying in type and degree of severity later in life, can continue to cause considerable disruption.

Although the progression of AD/HD into adolescence and adulthood is a new area of scientific research, there is a growing body of research suggesting that AD/HD which goes undetected and untreated in children may progress into more serious conditions, including: oppositional defiant disorder (ODD), conduct disorder (CD), and anti-social personality (all diagnoses distinct from AD/HD). For example, research has shown that over 65 per cent of children with AD/HD also display symptoms of ODD.

The projected developmental course of untreated AD/HD into adulthood is not positive. Without intervention, as years go by, the 'difficult' child with AD/HD-related family problems, peer rejection, academic failure and decreasing self-esteem appears to be at significant risk for developing into a maladjusted adult, who still carries the primary problems, embellished by layers of additional problems.

Theory and practice in the assessment of adult AD/HD is presently 'under construction' by researchers and clinicians. Unlike children, who are most often identified and referred by parents and teachers, adults with AD/HD are mostly self-referred. Because true AD/HD is inherited, not acquired later in life, the presence of symptoms in childhood is central to adult diagnosis. Typically, adults bring into assessment long histories of emotional and behavioural difficulties, which may have gone undiagnosed or, most often, misdiagnosed. High rates of divorce, depression, alcoholism, drug abuse, occupational failure, social isolation and, sometimes, criminality, appear to overlap with AD/HD over a lifetime, although more research must be done. By the time an adult is being considered for the

AD/HD diagnosis, the problem may well be compounded so that it is extremely difficult to differentiate primary causes from secondary problems, e.g. depression causing some AD/HD symptoms, or AD/HD over time causing depression.

Treatment approaches for adults diagnosed with AD/HD are not currently well developed. Research into effectiveness of the multimodal strategies recommended for children is being carried out. Regardless, enough is now known to recommend the value of early identification, diagnosis and intervention in an effort to prevent the development of multiple, compounding problems with the passage of time. Such an approach would appear to greatly improve the chances of an individual with AD/HD to lead a more fulfilling and productive life, at whatever age or stage.

Culture and AD/HD

In the 1960s and 1970s proponents of the 'anti-psychiatry' movement in the USA and Europe suggested that mental illness does not really exist. This radical assertion reflected cultural changes taking place worldwide, in which traditional, authoritarian structures and processes were challenged — and in many cases — overthrown by liberalism. The spread of democratic ideologies emphasising individual rights and the human rights of previously oppressed groups led some social activists to denounce ways in which western societies have dealt with issues of human differences.

The movement asserted that society creates mental illness in order to control and marginalise individuals considered undesirable. This movement had both positive and negative outcomes, many of which we encounter when exploring the relationship between culture and the AD/HD diagnosis. A powerful and positive effect of this movement was to humanise the treatment of people with mental illnesses and to diminish the stigma attached to it. A negative effect has been to create an aversion to biological and genetic explanations for mental and behavioural problems.

With this background in mind the present authors (Cooper and Ideus, 1995) carried out a study to establish the different cultural perspectives that are held about AD/HD in the UK and the USA. It is suggested that these preferences for particular perspectives are likely to be associated with particular preferences in terms of intervention or response.

An extensive literature search coupled with interviews with professionals (teachers, physicians and psychologists) produced the following eight orientations towards AD/HD:

1. *Moral Ethical*. This is the idea that the behaviours associated with AD/HD represent wilful and deliberate anti-social behaviour. In its extreme form, this view states that biological and or psycho-social explanations provide mere excuses for these problems, and are symptomatic of an amoral society where no one is prepared to be accountable for their actions. A more moderate position asserts that concepts like AD/HD can inhibit individuals' sense of autonomy, self efficacy and responsibility for their own behaviour.

2. *Allopathic-Medical*. This is the idea that AD/HD is primarily a medical problem, caused by a neurological dysfunction of some kind. In its extreme form this view opposes notions of environmental influence in

favour of a crude biological determinism. More moderate proponents of this view emphasise the way in which biological factors can create predispositions for certain difficulties, which are exacerbated or triggered by particular environmental factors. In this view the use of medication, whether it works or not, is seen as a soft option.

3. *Political-Ideological*. This view asserts that the AD/HD concept has been created to serve a social control function in favour of environmental and social constructionist explanations. This is the anti-psychiatry view in its extreme form, which is set up to challenge extremes of biological determinism. A more moderate form of this position states a concern for the way in which the diagnosis may be selectively misused in order to marginalise certain troublesome individuals.

4. *Pragmatism*. This is the view that accepts the diagnosis at face value. An extreme form of this position is totally unquestioning of the scientific underpinnings of the diagnosis, taking the view: 'If that's what scientists say the condition is then that is what it must be.' This view then accepts whatever 'expert' advice is given about the condition and how to deal with it. A more moderate version of this position takes the form of a guarded acceptance of the expert opinion, allowing reservations to be held in reserve until disproven. The common core to the pragmatic position is the tendency to focus on the solutions that the AD/HD diagnosis offers: 'if the treatment works then don't ask questions why!'

5. *Holistic-Medical*. This is the approach that sees AD/HD largely in terms of an allergic response to dietary or environmental toxins. Natural and therapeutic interventions are preferred in this orientation that seek to restore the suffering individual to a state of natural 'wholeness'. This orientation tends to be characterised by a resistance to allopathic-medical approaches which it sees as unnatural and potentially harmful as well as misguided.

6. *Cognitive Style*. This view asserts that AD/HD is not a disorder at all but simply an expression of individual differences in cognitive style of creativity. In its extreme forms this view is associated with the idea that people with AD/HD are in fact superior to the majority of people by virtue of their condition, and that the negative treatment they receive is a product of jealousy and ignorance. Moderate positions within this orientation stress the similarities between the traits of AD/HD and those of certain cognitive styles and creativity. This approach tends to favour environmental and educational explanations.

7. *Sociocultural*. The essence of this position is that there is nothing intrinsically 'disordered' about the traits associated with AD/HD. They are made dysfunctional by the ways in which they are culturally and socially interpreted. Thus, for example, hyperactivity is only made a problem in a culture where value is placed on docility and immobility. Furthermore, some of the behaviours associated with AD/HD may be socially produced, in that they are the product of labelling or the self-fulfilling prophecy. In its extreme form, this position holds that AD/HD is entirely a social construction, as is the biological research that underpins it. A more moderate position recognises the validity of the physiological research, but emphasises the social value that is placed on

the behavioural characteristics associated with AD/HD.

8. *Systematic-Eclectic*. This view attempts to synthesise many of the above positions in a systematic way. This view stresses the multifaceted nature of AD/HD, seeing it as a phenomenon that combines: biological, psychological, sociological and cultural aspects. This view is critical of any approach which seeks to diminish the importance of any one of these factors. This is the position that is held by the authors of this book.

We suggest that these different and sometimes conflicting views each produce different responses to the condition in terms of 'treatment' and other actions. It is vitally important therefore, for people to be aware of the particular orientation(s) they have in relation to AD/HD and to consider the effects of this.

AD/HD, cooperation and conflict

As we have already shown, much of what we know about the problems associated with AD/HD is concerned with conflict between people, in the classroom and in the home. Similarly, much of what we know about how best to deal with AD/HD depends on cooperation, among teachers, students parents and other professionals. Unfortunately, whilst teachers may find it comparatively easy to work in cooperative ways with students, other adults can pose problems.

Teachers, like most professionals are used to working with their student clients in private settings, with minimal interference from non-teaching professionals (except when they have OFSTED inspections). Teachers also have their own professional cultures, customs and practices that may sometimes lead to conflict. Teachers sometimes engage in demarcation disputes, when they feel they are being asked to do things which are outside their area of responsibility. They may have particular views and beliefs that make it difficult for them to cooperate with psychologists, medical doctors or parents. For example, they may have strong objections to the idea that behavioural problems can be influenced by biological factors.

These kinds of problems do not have an easy solution. What is important, however, for all adults and professionals involved in this kind of multidisciplinary exercise is to consider the primary purpose of the exercise: which is to serve the needs and interests of the child. In the case of a complex issue like AD/HD, it is important that teachers and others involved respect the opinions and expertise of each other. It is the responsibility of each member of the interdisciplinary team (including the parent) to attempt to understand the perspective of other professionals and to be open in communicating their own perspective.

Given that conflict is usually antithetical to the child's needs, the most important questions to ask, however, in any conflict situation are:

'What can I do to reduce the level of conflict?'
What can I do to improve the quality of effective and positive communication between myself and other members of the team?'

The second question can often be dealt with through the deployment of a short, polite and collegial letter or phone call, which addresses issues of concern whilst asserting a willingness and intention to cooperate. More serious problems may have to be addressed in face to face meetings.

School policies

Individual teachers are limited in what they can achieve on their own in any educational situation. They can be helped or hindered by the ways in which their schools are run. As suggested in Chapter 3, in relation to AD/HD there are many factors of school policy that will have the effect of either exacerbating or alleviating stress on children with AD/HD. Things like:

- school SEN policy;
- school discipline/behaviour policy;
- school policy on differentiation;
- homework policy;
- policies and preferences determining teaching styles and approaches;
- policies and practices relating to the use of medication in the school;
- pastoral arrangements;
- timetabling;
- environmental factors;
- arrangements for acknowledging achievement, and
- INSET priorities.

Other factors, which might be more loosely labelled as 'ethos', include:

- opportunities for student involvement in lessons and school life in general (formal and informal);
- governor, staff and student attitudes towards student differences, educational and behavioural problems;
- staff support mechanisms;
- degree to which parents feel welcome in the school;
- arrangements for parent consultation, and
- attitudes to visiting professionals.

National Education Policy

There is not enough space in this short book to deal with issues of educational policy in any detail. What is clear, however, is that some of the problems created by AD/HD lead to some fundamental questions about our current educational policy. Some examples follow.

- How appropriate is the National Curriculum in meeting the educational needs of all children, in terms of its content, structure and assessment procedures? To what extent do these arrangements allow all children to demonstrate their abilities and fulfil their attainment capacities?
- To what extent does the relative underfunding of primary schools, and the underfunding of schools in general work against the interests of children with learning difficulties?
- A direct result of these funding issues is the rise in class sizes. This has been accompanied by exhortations from the government and the chief HMI to increase the amount of 'whole class teaching in schools'. These measures are clearly, very likely to make the plight of children with difficulties (such as AD/HD) more serious, and, in turn affect the learning environment of their class-mates.
- The massive rise in school exclusion documented over recent years must

be seen as a threat to children who have AD/HD. What incentive do schools have to succeed with children who are not academically successful and potentially disruptive in a climate that judges schools primarily on the basis of examination results? Are OFSTED equipped to identify effective teaching for children with difficulties like AD/HD in mainstream schools?

- Are teachers effectively prepared in their Initial Training to meet the needs of children with difficulties like AD/HD in schools? Is the current one-year Post Graduate Certificate of Education an adequate and appropriate preparation for teachers? Is the increasing shifting of emphasis from the college to the school in delivering initial training appropriate? (See next point.)
- Is there sufficient funding for and access to appropriate INSET for experienced teachers to help them to sharpen and improve their skills?
- Is existing SEN legislation adequate, in guiding parents and the education service towards the means of meeting the needs of children with learning difficulties? Is it time to modify the current non-categorical system, by introducing reference to particular conditions and disorders?

Summary

- AD/HD is not an excuse for anything; AD/HD is real. AD/HD is a valuable tool that provides us with information that enables us to help particular children with serious educational and adjustment problems.
- There are many different ways of thinking about AD/HD, all of which have different implications for response and treatment.
- AD/HD for many people is a life-long condition.
- There are specific gender issues to be considered in relations to AD/HD. At the present time girls with AD/HD and nonhyperactive boys are at risk of having their problems ignored.
- AD/HD demands multidisciplinary/multiprofessional cooperation. Unfortunately this creates opportunities for conflict. It is essential that measures be taken to reduce conflict and maximise effective communication
- School Policies need to be developed that support the school's endeavours with AD/HD and related problems. Teachers cannot be expected to deal with these problems on their own.
- Schools' efforts to support their teachers, they must in turn be able to rely on the support of government. AD/HD — like all learning problems — is a problem shared by all of us.

QUESTIONS

1. What kinds of disagreements might AD/HD give rise to in your staffroom?

2. What might be done to resolve these arguments in ways that are sensitive to the needs of everyone involved?

3. What has been your experience of working with (a) parents and (b) other professionals and what implications does this have for dealing with AD/HD?

4. How might your school policies and ethos be improved (IF AT ALL) in the light of AD/HD?

5. What are we going to do about the government?

References

Cooper, P and Ideus, K (1995), 'Attention deficit disorder: sociocultural issues in assessment,' paper presented at the annual meeting of the American Educational Research Association, San Francisco, April, 1995

Jordan, D (1992), *Attention Deficit Disorder: ADHD and ADD Syndromes*, Austin, TX, Pro-Ed

Appendix A: Diagnostic Criteria

Table A1.1. Criteria for Attention Deficit/Hyperactivity Disorder

A.1. Inattention: At least six of the following symptons of inattention have persisted for at least 6 months to a degree that is maladaptive and inconsistent with developmental level.

a. Often fails to give close attention to details or makes careless mistakes in schoolwork, work, or other activities.

b. Often has difficulty sustaining attention in tasks or play activities.

c. Often does not seem to listen to what is being said to him or her.

d. Often does not follow through on instructions and fails to finish schoolwork, chores, or duties in the workplace (not due to oppositional behaviour or failure to understand instructions).

e. Often has difficulty organising tasks and activities.

f. Often avoids or expresses reluctance about, or has difficulties in engaging in tasks that require sustained effort (such as schoolwork or homework).

g. Often loses things necessary for tasks or activities (e.g., school assignments, pencils, books, tools or toys).

h. Is often easily distracted by extraneous stimuli.

A.2. Hyperactivity-Impulsivity: At least five of the following symptoms of hyperactivity-impulsivity have persisted for at least 5 months to a degree that is maladaptive and inconsistent with developmental level:

Hyperacitivty

a. Often fidgets with hands or feets or squirms in seat.

b. Leaves seat in classroom or in other situations in which remaining seated is expected.

c. Often runs about or climbs excessively in situations where it is inappropriate (in adolescents or adults, may be limited to subjective feelings of restlessness).

d. Often has difficulty playing or engaging in leisure activities quietly.

e. Is always 'on the go' and acts as if driven by a motor

f. Often talks excessively.

Impulsivity

g. Often blurts out answers to questions before they have been completed.

h. Often has difficulty waiting in lines or waiting in games or group situations.

B. Some symptoms that cause impairment were present before age 7.

C. Some symptoms that cause impairment must be present in two or more settings (e.g., at school, work, and at home)

D. There must be clear evidence of clinically significant impairment in social, academic or occupational functioning.

E. Does not occur exclusively during the course of a Pervasive Developmental Disorder, Schizophrenia or other Psychotic Disorder, or a Personality Disorder.

From *The Diagnostic and Statistical Manual of Mental Disorders* (DSM IV) (1993). Washington DC, American Psychiatric Association.

Table A1.2. Hyperkinetic Syndrome

A. Demonstrate abnormality of attention and activity at *home*, for the age and developmental level of the child, as evidenced by at least three of the following attention problems.

1. Short duration to spontaneous activities.
2. Often leaving play activities unfinished.
3. Overfrequent changes between activities.
4. Undue lack of persistence at tasks set by adults.
5. Unduly high distractibility during study, (e.g., homework or reading assignment); and by at least two of the following.
6. Continuous motor restlessness (running, jumping, etc).
7. Markedly excessive fidgeting or wriggling during spontaneous activities.
8. Markedly excessive activity in situations expecting relative stillness (e.g., mealtimes, travel, visiting church).
9. Difficulty in remaining seated when required.

B. Demonstrate abnormality of attention and activity at *school* or *nursery* (if applicable), for the age and development level of the child, as evidenced by at least two of the following attention problems.

1. Undue lack of persistence at tasks.
2. Unduly high distractibility, i.e., often orienting towards extrinsic stimuli.
3. Overfrequent changes between activities when choice is allowed.
4. Excessively short duration of play activities, and by at least two of the following activity problems.
5. Continuous and excessive motor restlessness (running, jumping, etc.) in school.
6. Markedly excessive fidgeting and wriggling in structured situation.
7. Excessive levels of off-task activity during tasks.
8. Unduly often out of seat when required to be sitting.

C. Directly observed abnormality of attention or activity. This must be excessive for the child's age and development level. The evidence may be any of the following.

1. Direct observation of the criteria in A or B above, i.e., not solely the report of parent and/or teacher.
2. Observation of abnormal levels of motor activity, or off-task behaviour, or lack of persistence in activities, in a setting outside home or school (e.g., clinic or laboratory).
3. Significant impairment of performance on psychometric test of attention.

D. Does not meet criteria for pervasive developmental disorder, mania, depressive or anxiety disorder

E. Onset before the age of six years.

F. Duration of at least six months.

G. IQ above 50.

The research diagnosis of Hyperkinetic disorder requires the definite presence of abnormal levels of inattention and restlessness that are pervasive across situations and persistent over time, that can be demonstrated by direct observation, and that are not caused by other disorders such as autism or affective disorders.

Eventually, assessment instruments should develop to the point where it is possible to take a quantitative cut-off score on reliable, valid, and standardised measures of hyperactive behaviour in the home and classroom, corresponding to the 95th percentile on both measures. Such criteria would then replace A and B above.

From the International Classification of Diseases (10th ed.) by the World Health Organisation, 1990, Geneva. Copyright 1990 by the World Health Orgnisation

Appendix B: Glossary of AD/HD-related terms

Assessment

A process including identification and evaluation of behaviours, difficulties, problems, traits, symptoms to determine whether or not AD/HD is present in a given individual. The process is conducted as an interdisciplinary effort to include the child, parents, physician, teachers, social workers and others having first-hand knowledge of both AD/HD, including its main features and diagnostic criteria, and the individual suspected of having the condition. Assessment involves collecting and pooling relevant information, followed by analysis which may or may not lead to assignment of a diagnosis.

Assesment Team

The presence or absence of AD/HD in an individual cannot be ascertained reliably by one person, not even a doctor. The condition is not assessed by a single medical test, but through careful, detailed exploration and analysis of long-term patterns of specific behavioural and emotional difficulties. Information shared by a group (team) of informed individuals is the basis of assessment and diagnosis. This group is the assessment team.

Attention Deficit Disorder

A medical diagnosis of the American Psychiatric Association (APA) used to describe a syndrome of emotional and behavioural difficulties experienced by children and adults which often results in lifelong emotional and behavioural difficulties in the home, school and workplace. Core features include extreme levels of impulsivity, inattentiveness and motoractivity, although not everyone shows all symptoms to the same degree. Three subtypes are currently recognised: (1) ADD with hyperactivity (the 'impulsive-hyperactive' type), (2) ADD without hyperactivity (the 'inattentive-impulsive type'), and (3) ADD-'residual' type, found in adults whose childhood symptoms persist after adolescence.

Diagnosis

An official statement of the presence of a medically verified condition.

Diagnostic Criteria

A standardised list of behaviours that indicate, at an early stage (before age seven), in extreme levels (compared with peers), and when displayed chronically (over six months) the presence of ADD/ADHD in an individual. The criteria form the standard against which teachers, parents, physicians and others interacting closely with the child over time, measure the individual's problems and difficulties. They are used to assess the presence or absence of AD/HD.

Dose Response

The general properties of psychostimulant medications have been well studied, giving rise to the 'dose response' concept used in the AD/HD field. This term refers to the fact that, in addition to the individualised responses unique to each child, research shows that some aspects of medication response are quite predictable, even systematic, when viewed 'across' differing dosage levels. Thus, at different dosages, different results are obtained in relation to eliminating or diminishing different AD/HD symptoms/problems. (see also *Individual medication responsivity*)

Evaluation

Synonym for the term assessment. Both refer to the process through which an individual's symptoms, traits, characteristics are identified, analysed and classified in order to determine whether or not the condition of AD/HD is present, leading to formal diagnosis.

Hyperactivity

One of the three core features of AD/HD, although not always present. A chronic, intense state of physical restlessness and motor overactivity not readily inhibited through conscious effort. Social, emotional and academic disruptiveness to self and others is associated with this problem

Hyperkinetic Syndrome (Hyperkinesis)

The term used by the World Health Organisation to describe chronic, extreme levels of motor activity in children when compared with 'normal' peers. Now recognised as a subtype of AD/HD, in that almost all hyperactive children also have impulse control and attention problems, although not all those with AD/HD are hyperactive.

Inattention

One of the three core features of AD/HD. Reduced ability to concentrate/focus on a task. Although the name AD/HD implies 'attention deficits' represent the *primary* problem underlying the syndrome, some experts now argue that impulse control 'deficits' are the core problem, as the impulse to act interferes directly with the ability to pay attention.

Individual Medication Responsivity

Although a medication is prescribed because research shows it has proven results in areas where improvement is needed, its actual results will depend to some degree on unique characteristics of the indivudal taking it. Thus, because research has shown stimulants to reduce AD/HD symptoms in 70–80 per cent of treated children studied, physicians expect a verifiable reduction in symptoms *in most cases*. However, whether or not a given child responds well, negatively or not at all depends on 'individual medication responsivity' related to the medication and dosage levels.

Impulsivity

One of the three core features of AD/HD. A neurological predisposition to act primarily without prior reflection or anticipation of consequences. Some theorists now believe it to be the *primary* underlying symptom, rather than hyperactivity as previously thought.

Medication Therapy

The use of medication as one component of treatment for AD/HD symptom reduction/elimination. Most commonly used medication therapy is methylphenidate, a stimulant, and sometimes, antidepressants are also used.

Methylphenidate

A stimulant medication chemically similar to the naturally occuring neurotransmitter, Dopamine. It is not an amphetamine, and appears to act by increasing levels of dopamine and norepinephrine in the brain. It is commonly prescribed under the brand name: 'Ritalin'.

Neurotransmitter

Chemical mediators in the brain responsible for transmitting electrical impulses from neuron to neuron, and neuron to muscle. The basic mechanism is such that a nervous impulse travels down the nerve axon until it reaches a synapse, triggering the release of the neurotransmitter, which in turn acts as a chemical 'bath' filling in the synaptic gap, thus allowing the impulse to pass. Deficits in production of four neurotransmitters (tyrosine, dopa, dopamine, and norepinephrine) appear to underly AD/HD.

Titrate (Titration)

Monitoring and adjusting the effects of medication, to produce desired outcomes/to reduce unwanted side effects. Establishing the correct medication dosage through observation of the effects produced by progressively increased dosages. Common practice in treating AD/HD is to begin with a low dose, which is then evaluated through observation for effectiveness in reducing or eliminating symptoms.

Appendix C: Selected further reading on AD/HD and the education of children with emotional and behavioural problems

Barkley, R.A. (1990), *Attention Deficit Hyperactivity Disorder: A Handbook for Diagnosis and Treatment*. New York: The Guilford Press.

Cooper, P.W. (1995), *Helping Them to Learn: Curiculum Entitlement For Children With EBD*, Stafford: NASEN

Cooper, P.W. and Ideus, K.M. (Eds.). (1994), *Attention Deficit/Hyperactivity Disorder: Educational, Medical and Cultural Issues*. East Sutton, Kent. The Association of Workers for Children with Emotional and Behavioural Difficulties.

DuPaul, G.J. and Stoner, G. (1995), *AD/HD in the Schools: Assessment and Intervention Strategies*. New York: The Guilford Press.

Goldstein, S. and Goldstein, M. (1990), *Managing Attention Disorders in Children. A Guide for Practitioners*. New York: Wiley.

Goldstein, S. and Goldstein, M. (1992), *Hyperactivity: Why Won't my Child Pay Attention?* New York: Wiley.

Hallowell, E.M. and Ratey, J.J. (1994), *Driven to Distraction. Recognising and Coping with Attention Deficit Disorder from Childhood through Adulthood*. London: Touchstone Books (Simon and Schuster).

Smith, C.J. and Laslett, R. (1993), *Effective Classroom Management: A Teacher's Guide* (2nd ed.). London: Routledge.

Train, A (1996), *AD/HD: How to Deal with Very Difficult Children*. London: Souvenir Press.

Wheldall, K. and Glynn, T. (1989), *Effective Classroom Learning*. Oxford: Blackwell.

Appendix D: Where to find help (Information, Assessment, Advocacy and Support Groups)

ADD Information Services
PO Box 340
Edgware
Middlesex HA8 9HL
Tel: (0181) 905 2013
Fax: (0181) 386 6466

ADD/ADHD Support Group (London)
88 Penshurst Gardens
Edgware, Middx., HA8 9TU
Tel: (0181) 958 6727

ADD-ADHD Family Support Group
1a High Street
Dilton Marsh
Westbury, Wilts.
BA13 4DL
Tel: (01373) 826045

or
93 Avon Road
Devizes, Wilts.
SN10 1PT
Tel: (01380) 726 710

AFASIC
347 Central Markets
Smithfield, London EC1A 9NH
Tel: (0171) 236 362/6487

Association of Workers for Children with Emotional and Behavioural
Difficulties (AWCEBD)
20 Carlton Street
Kettering, Northants NN16 8EB
Tel/Fax: (01536) 5518455

British Dyslexia Association
National Organisation for Specific Learning Difficulties
98 London Road
Reading, Berkshire RG1 5AU
Tel: (01734) 662677
Fax: (01734) 351927

Canadian Association for Children with Learning Difficulties
Kildare House
323 Chapel Street
Ottawa
Ontario KIN 7Z2
Tel: (603) 238-5721

Children and Adults With Attention Deficit Disorders (CHADD)
1859 North Pine Island Road, Suite 185
Plantation, FL 33322 USA
Tel: (305) 587-3700

LADDER
National Learning and Attention Deficit Disorders Association
142 Mostyn Road
London SW19 3LR
Tel: (0181) 543 2800
Fax: (0181) 543 4800
or 95 Church Road
Bradmore
Wolverhampton WV3 7EW

The Mental Health Foundation
37 Mortimer Street
London W1N 8JU
Tel: (0171) 580 0145
Fax: (0171) 631 3868

The Tavistock and Portman NHS Trust
Child and Family Department
Tavistock Clinic
120 Belsize Lane
London NW3 5BA
Tel: (0171) 435 7111

Tourette Syndrome Associates
42–40 Bell Boulevard
Bayside, New York 10016 USA
Tel: (718) 224-2999

University of Massachusetts
Department of Psychiatry
University of Massachusetts Medical Center
Attention Deficit Hyperactivity Disorder Clinic
55 Lake Avenue North
Worcester, MA 01655-0239 USA
Tel: (508) 8956-2552
Fax: (508) 856-3595

Index